# Light and Hope
## Methodist Prayer Handbook 2013/2014

*Primavera Quantrill,
Editor (Juliet Piper)*

Two hundred years ago, just before his death in 1814, Thomas Coke founded the third Methodist mission, in Ceylon (now Sri Lanka).

Methodist mission overseas had begun in 1786 when Coke, driven off course by a storm, landed in Antigua. Within a few years, the mission had reached almost every British colony in the West Indies.

In 1811, not deterred by earlier failures in Africa, Coke began a new, successful, mission to Sierra Leone.

Through brave and hopeful men and women like Coke, the light of Christ is now celebrated in all parts of the world. Whereas a hundred years ago 80% of the world's Christians lived in Europe and North America, now 60% live in Asia, Africa and Latin America.*

Christian hope is not just about praying that something good will happen in the future, but laying a first brick, planting a first seed, teaching a child a new song even if you won't be the one to live in the house or gather the fruit from the tree or hear that song become an anthem that will be chanted around the world.

*Primavera Quantrill, Editor*

## Praying around the world

I am often asked how we choose the countries to represent in the Methodist Prayer Handbook. They are countries where the Methodist Church in Britain has Church-to-Church relationships. This reflects the origins of the Handbook, which was originally a booklet of prayers for the overseas districts of the British Methodist Church and places wherein the Methodist Missionary Society was engaged. Over the years this further expanded to cover 'home' districts as well as the districts of the Methodist Church in Ireland. You might want to look at the map in the inside back cover and 'pray around the world' for those countries without a formal Methodist presence.

**Prayer Handbook Committee**

Norman Wallwork (chair)
Sarah Bennison
Jenny Ellis
David Friswell
Suzanne Johnson
Ken Kingston
Primavera Quantrill

**Editing and typesetting**

Primavera Quantrill

*Todd M. Johnson and Kenneth R. Ross (eds), Atlas of Global Christianity (Edinburgh University Press, 2009)

## Prayer of hope

God of abundant joy,
help us to see you in the life we live,
to recognise you in ordinariness
and to celebrate your extraordinary love.

God of generous giving,
help us to share your extravagant grace,
to care deeply about the lives of others
and to offer hope where there is despair.

God of endless mercy,
help us to know we are forgiven and loved,
to welcome your healing power to change
and to live in harmony on this earth today.

God of bountiful love,
help us to shout out the good news of Jesus
to reawaken the desire of our hearts
and connect again
with your Spirit of peace. Amen.

*Alison Richards, minister, Malvern*

Lord Jesus Christ,
Illuminate the dark places in our world.
Give peace where there is unrest,
Hope where there is despair,
Trust where there is suspicion.

Amid all the uncertainties of life today
Nothing is surer than the
Dependability of your love, so

Help us, in joyful hope, to
Overcome our fear and
Prepare ourselves for service, as we
Embrace your light. Amen.

*Margaret Bickerdike, Bexhill-on-Sea*

HoPE For People Who ARe Being Bullied
HOPE For Parents Who Have Lost there Children
HOPE For People Who are Home-Less
HOPE For People Who are in Hospital
HOPE For People Who have no money
HOPE For People Who have being flooded
HOPE FOr the world and Peace!
Amen!

*Tallis Keeler, aged 10, St Andrew's Methodist Primary School, Manchester*

Lord God, we thank you for
the first signs of the waking world at springtime,
for the signs of hope for the year ahead.
Where once was brown earth, we see green shoots.
In the shade shines the frosted brilliance of snowdrops
and dark afternoons lengthen into later sunsets.

*The frosted brilliance of snowdrops (Alan Barker)*

Help us to see you, too, in unexpected places;
your presence making the ordinary extraordinary,
so we may turn to you with renewed love and trust each day.
We ask this for Jesus' sake. Amen.

*Catherine James, local preacher, Derby*

God of hope, in whom there is no darkness at all,
fill our lives with your light and illuminate our thinking,
that we may reflect your light in the dark places of our world today.
Use us to bring about:
    love where there is hatred and bitterness;
    hope where there is negative thinking;
    encouragement where there is ignorance and lack of purpose.
May your light reach out to every person we encounter,
that each one may recognise you, and come to know you,
the source of all light and hope and love. Amen.

*Hazel Eagle, Stoneleigh*

From the desperation of poverty and the shadows of injustice we pray, Lord,
that you will cast out darkness and burst in with light upon your world.
Answer the cries of our prayers:
    light and hope;
    justice and freedom;
    health and prosperity;
    life in all its fullness.
Strengthen our faith, hope and love as we look towards better days.
Lord, hear our prayer. Amen.

*Srijana Holland, aged 16, daughter of mission partners, Togo*

God is with us always: may we feel his presence on both dark and bright days.

*Ana Palik-Kunčak, Superintendent, Serbia*

God, you are the light for our path
and the joy in our hearts,
the hope in our lives and in our world.
We praise your holy name
and rejoice in your love and protection.
Grant that we may always keep our eyes fixed on you
and that our lives may bring joy to your heart. Amen.

*Beryl Wakefield, Nuthall Methodist Church*

*(© Anya Goldsack, used with permission)*

Loving God,
when I look at the earth which you have created,
I see your mighty power and your tender gentleness.
I see your glory and your simplicity.
I see evidence of your sense of humour
and your caring provision for all your creation.
All that you have made tells me that this earth is held
in the hands of a loving and generous God. Amen.

*Joan Ungemuth, Bromley Common Methodist Church*

*(Heather Rushton)*

Glorious God,
maker of heaven and earth,
morning star at the beginning of our days,
guiding and leading us onwards,
leaving darkness behind,
we adore you.

Jesus, light of the world,
bright sun, chasing shadows,
providing light and energy,
all we need to grow, to thrive,
we praise you.

Flaming Spirit,
warming and strengthening,
fanning the embers of our service,
bringing us peace as evening draws nigh,
we thank you. Amen.

*Jean Murrie, supernumerary minister,*
*Angus, Dundee and Perthshire Circuit*

Almighty God,
strong and powerful,
unique and invincible,
we live to honour you.

You are the King of glory.
You are the one who made heaven
and the earth
and everything in it.
You are our consolation and our saviour.
You are our strength and our song.
Before you, in you and through you,
with open hearts and minds,
we are ready to receive the seeds
of care and love,
to go out to sow compassion and healing
to our war-weary world.
You are so welcome here with us today,
our special King of glory. Amen.

*Andrea Sheppick,*
*Shropshire and the Marches Circuit*

O God,
it is so easy to lose sight of your kingdom,
so easy to clutter life up
and make the simple complicated.

Lead us to the simplicity of life with you,
open our eyes and show us
how near we are to your kingdom
in everyday things.

Stop us from falling into
rich young man syndrome,
and from being
so rich, so religious, so clever
that we lose sight of you,
our simple, gracious, loving God.

Grant us the grace
to set our inner child free,
for we ask this in the name of the one who
welcomed the children. Amen.

*Audrey Hensman,*
*local preacher, Inverness*

Lord God, how can we call you 'Father',
if we do not call one another
'sister' and 'brother'?

How can we turn and face you,
if we turn our backs and our hearts
against those whom you also love?

How can we recognise your love,
if we cannot offer our love to those who
are different from ourselves?

Lord God, bring us all into your family,
hold us close to you and to each other.
Amen.

*Fiona Green,*
*local preacher, Ashbourne*

## Prayer for relationships

In gratitude to God
for giving people to me,
I name in prayer:
    those who have befriended me;
    those who have guided me;
    those who have nurtured me;
    those who have put up with me
    those who have supported me;
    those who have goaded me into action.

In penitence (simply saying sorry)
I name in prayer:
    those I dislike;
    those who irritate me;
    those I can't get on with,
        or find difficult to love
    those I have hurt.
And for myself, make me like Jesus, Lord.
Amen.

*John North, local preacher, Preston*

## Hope and Forgiveness

Lord, I am aware that within my life there
is much that mars my faith and profession.
I rejoice that there is hope even for me in
the salvation offered by Jesus. In hope, I
look to him for friendship, solace, comfort
and new strength to face adversity.

As I look to the end of my days, so I rejoice
in the hope of eternal life. I have reason
for hope that Jesus has cancelled my
sin by his death on the cross and by his
resurrection has shown me the hope of life
in your presence.

Forgive my sin, heavenly Father, and
assure me of the great hope that is mine
through the death and resurrection of
Jesus my Lord. Amen.

*From* Every Day Prayers for Everyday People
*Ray Cornick, local preacher,*
*Poole and Swanage Circuit*

We give you thanks, kindly God, for all your many and good gifts:

for the gift of wind and weather, sun and rain,
by which you nourish the earth so that it produces enough
    for the needs of all animals and people,
and through which you also send warnings of our misuse of your world;

for the gift of friends and family, neighbours and colleagues,
through whom you encourage us to nurture and care for each other,
and through whom you also warn us of the consequences of selfishness;

for the gift of your Word and the ability to read it in our own language,
through which you teach and guide us,
and through which you also challenge us to think for ourselves.

Help us ever to bear your gifts, your Word and your warnings in mind,
so that we learn your will for us all,
and thus keep alive our hope that your will may indeed be done. Amen.

*Rosi MorganBarry, local preacher, Berkshire Surrey Borders Circuit*

Loving God, we thank you for the bonds of friendship
which help to structure our lives.
We cannot do without them
any more than we can do without you.
So we pray:
hold us firm in faith, grounded in love,
and strengthen our ties and relationships,
so that we may become a safe haven for the lost
and a refuge for the dispossessed. Amen.

*Diane Coleman, local preacher
and Warden of Norwood Retreat Centre*

*The bonds of friendship
(Karen Drayton)*

*(Peter Barber)*

I worship and thank you, O Lord my God,
for the potential and wonder of each new day,
for the ordinary things, and the magnificent things,
for the glimpses of the divine,
    giving hope in times of darkness,
for the assurance of your presence, wherever I am,
for the promise of your love and mercy, every day,
for the opportunity to share what little I know of you,
and for the hunger to learn more.
And so I worship and thank you Lord, with all my heart. Amen.

*Lyn Gennoe, local preacher, Warwickshire*

Generous God,
we thank you that by your Spirit and through your Son
you have given gifts to your Church
by calling some of us to be apostles,
some prophets, evangelists, pastors and teachers
and all of us to works of service
and to the building up of the Body of Christ.

*Forward together in hope*
*(David Pepin)*

Help us to fulfil our ministries
and to encourage others in theirs,
that we may reach unity in the faith,
grow up into Christ, the head of the body,
and build each other up in love. Amen.

*based on Ephesians 4*
*Leo Osborn, Chair, Ministries Committee*

---

Lord God:
    make me leadable...
      ...and lead me;
    make me teachable...
      ...and teach me;
    make me usable...
      ...and use me;
for the sake of Jesus, my leader, teacher and master. Amen.

*Stephen Bales, supernumerary minister, St Ives and Hayle*

---

Creator God, everything you made, you pronounced to be very good.
We thank you that we have the same creativity within us.
We pray for the many that cannot express that creativity in work,
and feel frustrated, useless and bitter.
Loving Father God, by your Holy Spirit,
give them a sense of their own value,
hope for the future
and fulfilment in different ways of being creative.
As your willing disciples,
we offer ourselves as your agents
in bringing joy for the present and hope for the future.
In Jesus' name. Amen.

*Colin Smith, supernumerary minister, Sankey Valley Circuit*

7

Eternal God, we thank you
for the energy and vibrancy that children and young people bring to our world.
We thank you for their creativity and inquisitiveness.
We thank you that Jesus told the disciples to "let the children come to me".
We are sorry for those times when we, as individuals or as churches,
have stopped the children and young people around us coming close to Jesus.
We pray
> for children and young people for whom life seems complicated;
> for children with life-limiting conditions;
> for children struggling with eating disorders;
> for children who are self harming and those who have no self-esteem;
> for children who are not able to access education;
> for children who have been enlisted as soldiers;
> for children who do not have the basic needs of water, food or shelter.

Help us today to notice the children and young people around us,
and to give thanks for each and every one of them. In Jesus' name. Amen.

*Nicola Briggs, Youth and Children's Officer, Southampton District*

Transplanting God,
you suddenly shine a light in the darkened rooms of long illnesses and struggles.
You bring hope to birth in deepening weakness for those who desperately wait and pray.
You inspire donor families to offer new life from the deep pain of their grief and loss.
You empower and inspire clinicians and surgeons to make transplants possible.
You embrace those receiving transplants through the love of families and friends.
When life seems to be running out, you sometimes have other ideas.
For into darkened rooms the sunshine somehow finds a window.
Transplanting God, we celebrate your sign of hope in those who have had transplants
and in so many others who still wait. Amen.

*Michael Corney, recipient of a liver transplant, Norwich*

---

**A hospice prayer**
Loving God, we thank you for the assurance of your love shown to us in your Son,
Jesus Christ, and especially your compassion on those suffering from pain or fear.
We thank you for the privilege of working with you to bring help and comfort to the sick,
the dying and those who mourn, especially through the hospice movement.
Thank you for everyone who helps in any way to make this possible, and who continues
to support this ministry through prayer, giving or caring for patients.
Give wisdom, sensitivity and compassion to all who work together for the blessing of
patients and their relatives. Amen.

*Maurice Staton, chaplain, St Leonard's Hospice, York*

Help us, O Lord, to meet each morning with courage and hope,
to measure each day with love and laughter
and, at evening, to know your forgiveness and feel your blessing. Amen.

*Marian Evans, retired midwife and minister's wife, Swindon*

God of hope,
as I open my eyes in the morning,
I give you my first wakeful thoughts
for I know that my day depends on my hope in you.

God of light,
as I close my eyes in sleep,
I give you my last wakeful thoughts
for I know that your light shines in the darkness. Amen.

*Sunrise over Galilee
(Val Facey)*

*Donald Craig, Bradford North Circuit*

### When life is tough

May the Lord comfort us in sorrow,
calm us when anxious,
befriend us when lonely,
embolden us when afraid,
guide us with the light of his presence
and protect us with the golden wings
of his love. Amen.

*Annette Sampson,
local preacher, Birmingham*

### Dawn prayer

Gracious God,
as the first rays of light
creep across the skyline,
we ask that your light
may be with us this day,
and that the hope we have in you
will be with us always
until we meet with you in glory.
In the name of our risen Lord. Amen.

*June Dingwall, local preacher,
Exeter, Coast and Country Circuit*

Here, Lord, we stand
at the beginning of a new day.
Once you, too, Lord, stood like us,
perhaps not knowing
the way that you would take.
Even so, you journeyed on,
trusting in your Father's love.

So let us, too, go on in faith and hope,
into this day with all its joys,
its sorrows too, if need be,
guided on our way
by your Spirit's presence with us,
holding your hand, Lord,
and held in your light,
trusting you to bring us safe
to this day's end. Amen.

*Ron Dingwall, local preacher,
Exeter, Coast and Country Circuit*

## Praying with all creation

Come from the four winds, O Lord, and in your holiness breathe upon us with your Spirit, that we may be gathered into your kingdom; for yours is the glory and the power throughout all ages, world without end. Amen.

*The Didache (c.100)*

**Cosmic prayer**
Lord of vastness,
of colliding galaxies, of an ever-expanding universe,
we stand in awe at the magnificence of creation.
In all this vastness, our little planet.
On this vast planet, our little lives.
How small we are,
and yet you gave us minds vast enough to reach out,
to see the beauty of your plan
and the power of your arm. Amen.

*Annette Kupke, Stirling Methodist Church*

God of resurrection,
in our damaged lives and communities
your irresistible power is the ground of our hope.
You show profligate creativity and love
in a daily rhythm of darkness and dawn, rest and activity.
In a frenzied, competitive and violent world,
we remember that the work of salvation – new creation –
is your labour, not our effort.
You stir our creative response
and daily we create, let go, forgive,
pausing in awe to see
what new thing you are doing through us and others
to bless the world. Amen.

*Jenny Ellis, Coordinator of Evangelism,*
*Spirituality and Discipleship, Connexional Team*

Dear Lord, make us as wick as bugs on a hot oven plate.*

*A prayer by a old local preacher*
*used in a village chapel near Scarborough 100 years ago*
**Brian and Susan Thomas, Scarborough**

*(Andrea Sheppick,*
*Paul Martin, Andrea*
*Sheppick, Bob Faraway)*

*wick=lively

## A prayer for the Methodist Church in Britain

Almighty God,
in the beginning you made the world and saw that it was good,
yet today we see a world broken and in need of healing:
people face discrimination and injustice,
children live in poverty, hunger and disease,
and many are denied their basic human rights.
People cry out for justice: they want a better world,
where all can be valued and hope for life in all its fullness.
Your Son promised a world
that is healthy, just, inclusive and sustainable.
Give us courage to speak out and work for this new society.
Enable us to be agents of your kingdom,
in the name of Jesus Christ,
who taught us to pray: "Your kingdom come, your will be done,
on earth as in heaven." Amen.

*Daleep Mukarji,*
*Vice-President of the British Methodist Conference, 2013/2014*

---

God spoke –
and there was light.
God spoke –
and there was life.
Living Word,
speak into our lives,
that our words and works
might be life and light in the world. Amen.

*Ruth Gee,*
*President of the British Methodist Conference, 2013/2014*

---

Heavenly Lord, we ask you to continue to encourage, equip and enable the officers and the connexional forum of Methodist Women in Britain. May they give leadership and inspiration to all the women of the Church. Strengthen, we pray, their campaigns to shine light on areas of injustice so that your hope may become known to the poor, the marginalised and the powerless. Amen.

*Linda Crossley, President, Methodist Women in Britain*

**President of the British Methodist Conference**
Ruth Gee

**Vice-President**
Daleep Mukarji

**British Connexional Team**

**General Secretary/ Secretary of the Conference**
Martyn Atkins

**Assistant Secretary of the Conference**
Gareth Powell

**Connexional Secretary**
Doug Swanney

**Cluster Heads**
Gareth Hill
Jude Levermore
Nick Moore

**Warden of the Diaconal Order**
Sue Culver

**Youth President**
Tamara Wray

## Praying with Christians in West Africa

Grant us, O Lord, the will to accomplish all that pleases you; the strength to do all that you command and the reverence to respect all that you have made; for your own name's sake. Amen.

*Francis of Assisi (1182-1226)*

### The Gambia

**Bishop**
Hannah Faal-Heim

### Sierra Leone

**Methodist President**
Arnold Temple

**Mission Partners**
th Wendy° Kilworth-Mason
ad/m Michael and Joanna Tettey, Joelle and Janelle

*Lunchtime at the Bethel Nursery School, Banjul, The Gambia (Margaret Gardener)*

Almighty God, we give thanks for the Methodist Church **The Gambia** as it continues to be a beacon of light;
for the friendship it shares with its Muslim sisters and brothers and with national leaders and government;
for the dedication of the new church in Cassamance, Senegal, built by Gambian fishing families who have moved there and the rural church in Nyofellah in The Gambia built with the support of Methodists in Britain.
We pray for ecumenical partners in the Christian Council as they work closely together;
for the Prison Fellowship ministry that offers pastoral care and service to prisoners;
for lively centres of worship in urban and rural areas with large numbers of young people.

*Sarah Jason, former mission partner, The Gambia*

### A prayer for Sierra Leone

In the dry season, as the earth lies parched and bare
    and dust pervades everything, we hope for rain.
So when the storm clouds gather,
send the rains to freshen the heavy air,
to cleanse the atmosphere and wash the streets.

Fill the Bumbuna dam so that electricity can be generated
so that school children can have light by which to read
and work places, where hands and machines otherwise lie idle,
can use the power to enhance production and productivity.

Drench the earth, that the land may be fertile,
let there be food in abundance so that the people may eat.
Nourish your people in body and spirit.

Then, when the faithful gather in church, mosque
    or place of worship,
they will give thanks to God, the giver of all good things. Amen.

*Wendy Kilworth-Mason, mission partner, Sierra Leone*

We thank God for new initiatives of practical Christianity within the community, during these difficult economic times;
for the new Irish, who have joined congregations in the Dublin District, whose diversity and cultures bless churches with fresh expressions of worship and growing congregations.
We pray for Andrew Dougherty, the new district superintendent, that he may know the blessing of God's leadership and be filled with wisdom and grace in the Holy Spirit;
for the district as it seeks new ways to minister effectively in a changing landscape.

**Dublin District (Ireland)**

Superintendent
Andrew Dougherty

---

We give thanks for the Healthy Living Programme and ecumenical and inter faith relationships in the London District;
for pastoral and prophetic engagement in church and community through a range of chaplaincies;
for work with children and young people, supported by skilled and dedicated volunteers.
We pray for everyone in the London District who is responding to increasing poverty and homelessness;
for projects offering care in the name of the Church, which are often faced with complex funding and management issues;
for London, that its citizens might be bearers of God's light into places where hope hangs by a thread.

**London District**

Chairs
Jenny Impey
Stuart Jordan
Michaela Youngson

God, who is with us
in the midst of traffic chaos and noisy commerce,
remind us to stop and listen to the sounds of longing hearts.
In the dark loneliness of crowded living,
remind us to look for glimpses of your light.
When tempted to see only struggle and bad news,
remind us that the city is full of stories of hope and human flourishing.
Help us to be the human agents of your divine grace. Amen.

*Michaela Youngson, London District Chair*

Lord, please help me to bear patiently with the peculiarities of my friends ... and while you're about it, Lord, please help my friends to bear patiently with mine. Amen.

*Tony New, New River Circuit, London*

## Praying with Christians in West Africa

King of Glory, transform our wayward passions with the gift of your grace. Christ of Galilee, calm our raging storms with the command of your word. Shepherd of Bethlehem, comfort our fearful hearts with the sound of your voice. Amen.

*Clement of Alexandria (c.150-c.215)*

**Benin**

Methodist President
Nicodème Alagbada

Scholarship Students
Jeanne Agnila
Nounagnon Adolphe
 Zannou-Tchoko
Jeremie Kpedetin
 Gadanaou
Paul Tiburce Kpamegan
 (all in Cameroon)

**Côte d'Ivoire**

United Methodist
Bishop
Benjamin Boni

**Togo**

Methodist President
Charles Klagba

Mission Partners
p/ed Michael° and
 Sheila Holland,
 Srijana and Saffron

Scholarship Student
Ayité Enyonam Hillah
 (in Ghana)

We thank God for 170 years of Methodist mission in **Benin**, giving birth to the Protestant Methodist Church of Benin, which became an autonomous conference in March 1993; for the growth of the Church through the Training, Evangelism and Spirituality Programme and Volunteer Youth for Christ. We pray for peace and development in Benin and for peace and security for people and property in Africa, particularly in Mali, Nigeria, the Central African Republic and the Democratic Republic of Congo.

*Nicodème Alagbada, President,*
*Protestant Methodist Church of Benin*

We give thanks for 100 years of Methodism in **Côte D'Ivoire**; for Prophet William Harris through whom 200,000 people came to faith in 1913; for the completion of the Kouya New Testament, and for 25 years of dedication from Philip and Heather Saunders of Wycliffe Bible Translation, from Northern Ireland. We pray for the new Diaconal Training Centre; for CAHPA (Co-operative for Artists Handicapped Physically Abidjan) which gives men and women a sense of dignity through their work, enabling them to live with hope, that they may find new sales outlets for their crafts.

*Brian Griffin, Midlands and Southern*
*District Superintendent, Ireland*

We thank God that the Methodist Church in **Togo** is celebrating 170 years since the gospel arrived in Togo with the first Methodist missionaries. We pray that the God of history would heal the wounds caused consciously or in ignorance during the last 170 years of life together; that every Methodist in Togo would rededicate themselves to the Christian faith.

*Charles Klagba, President, Église Methodiste du Togo*

We give thanks for the newly stationed ministers, including the Western Area Assistant Chair, Conrad Hicks;
for those working in youth projects that give hope to young people, particularly the initiative in Egham where the post of Police Community Youth Pastor has been created;
for Messy Church, street pastors and other outreach and evangelism initiatives;
for leaders and their work with ecumenical partners, including the recently appointed Archbishop of Canterbury, Justin Welby;
for circuits which are taking on the challenges of the 'Unlocking the Growth' seminars.

---

*"The light shines in the darkness
and the darkness did not overcome it."* John 1:5

You are the God of dark matter and dazzling galaxies;
war-torn countries and growing economies;
broken communities and thriving neighbourhoods;
hidden thoughts and healthy conversations.
Pierce the shadows that surround
and threaten to overwhelm us with your light.
Bring the hope and joy of your Son
which can never be overcome. Amen.

*John Hellyer, South East District Chair*

---

God, loving guide, graciously, and at such cost,
you offer an invitation to all to follow you.

Stir, we pray, in every heart a longing for you:
grant us discernment that we may recognise your direction;
grant us courage that we may step out and follow;
grant us deep trust in you, loving God,
the one who holds and promises never to abandon us.

As we follow you, Lord God, we pray
that in the power of your Spirit,
you will illumine your people with your light,
that you will form the lives of those who commit to you,
that every aspect of our lives together will point to Jesus
and that your people will be a blessing to many. Amen.

*Heather Morris, President of the
Irish Methodist Conference 2013/2014*

## South East District

**Chair**
John Hellyer

**Assistant Chairs**
Conrad Hicks
Philip Luscombe
Rose Westwood

*Pierce the shadows ...
overwhelm us with your
light (© Anya Goldsack,
used with permission)*

## Irish Connexional Team

**President**
Heather Morris

**Lay Leader of the Conference**
Kenneth Twyble

**Secretary of the Conference**
Donald Ker

**Secretary of MMS (Ireland)**
Laurence Graham

**Home Mission Secretary**
Des Bain

Show us, O Lord, the transience of the world in the light of heaven, the shortness of time in the light of eternity and the meaning of death in the light of resurrection; through the merits of Christ the Lord. Amen.

*Richard Challoner (1691-1781)*

**Equatorial Guinea**

Methodist President
Norberto Dioso Bonde

**Ghana**

Methodist Presiding Bishop
Emmanuel Asante

Scholarship Student
Emmanuel Asamoh-
Okyere (in Britain)

We give thanks for the appointment of the Methodist Presiding Bishop of **Ghana**, Emmanuel Asante, as the chairman of the National Peace Council.
We pray for intensive evangelism and church growth in 2013 and beyond;
for Christian unity, religious tolerance and God's guidance for the new political leadership in Ghana.

*Methodist Church in Ghana*

Father God, we rejoice in the peace which your country Ghana has experienced over the years.
We pray that the new President, John Dramani Mahama and his government will have the wisdom to rule Ghana in such a manner that other countries will continue to respect Ghana's democratic process;
for a solution to ongoing corruption and injustice, that all Ghanaians may benefit from the wealth arising from Ghana's natural resources;
for good environmental management so that the livelihoods of farmers and fishermen will be protected.

*Diana Bosman, former mission partner, Ghana*

*Uphill struggles in Ghana (Ian Bosman)*

Father, we give thanks for all those called to serve you through the Methodist missionary societies over the past 200 years. We ask your blessings on the Methodist and Wesleyan Churches around the world as they share the gospel and bring people into a personal relationship with you. Give us hope for the future as we continue to respond to your call to go out into our neighbourhoods and the world to serve our sisters and brothers, that we may become a Church energised in mission for the glory of your name. Amen.

*David Friswell, World Church Relationships Team Leader*

We give thanks for the Midlands and Southern District which has grown in numbers by 25 per cent in recent years; for the faithful and dedicated ministers and local preachers, who every Sunday travel, sometimes over a hundred miles, to ensure God's word is proclaimed; for loyal members who maintain properties so they are comfortable for worship and suitable places for establishing relationships with the wider community; for the link with the world church which is made strong through regular prayer, giving and support for specific projects such as the Mary and Elizabeth movement in Egypt.

We pray for the new house church in South Tipperary where there has not been a Methodist witness for nearly 100 years; for the new Surf Pioneer Ministry, Lahinch, Co Clare, where young people encounter God in an unforced, creative and relevant way; for circuits facing financial challenges, who are coming together to look at new ways of being Church and using their human resources more effectively.

### Midlands and Southern District (Ireland)

**Superintendent**
Brian Griffin

*Ministry of surf (Andy Hill)*

---

We give thanks for the joy, enthusiasm and new ideas that probationers and those in their early years in ministry bring to the circuits and churches in their care; for community initiatives such as the De Havilland Project in Hatfield, the Grub Club in Clacton and the Community Café in Basildon.

We pray for worship leaders, local preachers, local tutors and the joint preacher training initiative between the Bedfordshire, Essex and Hertfordshire and East Anglia Districts; for pastoral visitors and those who support elderly, frail and vulnerable people in the community.

### Bedfordshire, Essex and Hertfordshire District

**Chair**
Anne Brown

> When we are going through dark times
> give us, O God, glimpses of light.
> May we never lose our hope and trust in you.
> Help us to remember that, however hard the path, however dark the tunnel,
> at the end of it is the light of your love beckoning us on. Amen.
> *Anne Brown, Bedfordshire, Essex and Hertfordshire District Chair*

# DAY 5

Shine upon us, O Lord, with the light that surpasses all other light. Cleanse us with the fire that consumes all other fires and fill us with the love that transforms all other loves; for your own name's sake. Amen.

*Catherine of Siena (c.1347-1380)*

## Nigeria

**Methodist Prelate**
Makinde Sunday
Olatunji

**Mission Partners**
p  Ros Colwill
d  Hans and Mary Van
den Corput, Marcel
and Maurice

## Cameroon

**Moderator of the
Presbyterian Church**
Festus Asana

**Mission Partners**
p/p  Daniel° and
Grace Pratt Morris-
Chapman, Kwame

**Scholarship Student**
Saibo Lamsin Nakeka
wa Dialle
(in Cameroon)

Ozuzu-Oke Retreat Centre teaches that life can flourish if only we are attentive to the presence of God in our lives. We join the world Methodist family in praying for flood victims in **Nigeria,** that they may find hope in Christ and reassurance that God still cares for them.

*Rosalind Faith Colwill, director, Ozuzu-Oke Retreat Centre*

Loving God, we thank you for the unity of **Nigeria,** despite the continuing domestic crisis;
for the growth of the Methodist Church Nigeria under the leadership until October 2013 of Dr Sunday Ola Makinde.
We pray for those who are involved in the ministry of reconciliation between people of different cultures and faiths;
for the new Prelate of the Methodist Church Nigeria elected in 2013;
for peace, justice and freedom of worship, especially in the Northern part of Nigeria.

*Amos Kayode Olu Ogunrinde,
Assistant Director of Evangelism and Discipleship, Nigeria*

Dear Lord, we pray for the situation in **Cameroon,** particularly for the elderly who are trying to raise grandchildren orphaned by HIV/AIDS.
We pray that the elderly who feel deserted and unable to help their grandchildren will feel your love and grace;
for those who are supporting this elderly generation by providing clubs and income-generating activities and that, with your blessing, these will be successful.
Lead us, in the security of the UK, to remember them in our prayers and our giving.

*Newbury Methodist Church, courtesy of MRDF*

We give thanks for our call to engage in the ministry of all God's people. We hold Ian and Barbara Howarth and their family in our prayers as Ian begins his ministry as the Chair of the Birmingham District.

We give thanks for daily expressions of love and faith in the lives of individuals and in churches in a wide variety of communities. We pray for people who are working to initiate and sustain our mission and ministry in challenging places.

We give thanks for the places of learning across the Birmingham District, where lives are enriched as people engage in the joy of finding new things. We pray for the work of the Queen's Foundation as it continues to work for the development of the ministry of the whole people of God.

**Birmingham District**

Chair
Ian Howarth

*Deacon Kerry Smith and Hattie Hodgson of the Adavu Project raising awareness of human trafficking with a UN Gift Cube in Birmingham's Victoria Square (Bill Anderson)*

> Great God of love, fill our lives with your hope:
> hope that gives birth to justice;
> hope that builds well-being in community;
> hope that reaches out hands to make peace;
> hope that finds expression in daily acts of love;
> and so your kingdom comes. Amen.
>
> *Bill Anderson, former Birmingham District Chair*

God of truth and mystery,
today your creature, light, blazes so brightly,
that I cannot quite decide
whether I am seeing with clarity or am half-blinded,
whether following your way is unmistakable
or even my very surety of you is a shimmering mirage:
guide me.

When your creature, dark, is come,
and I cannot quite decide
whether I am seeing anything clearly at all,
or whether the familiar dim outlines of things near and far
are as real and solid as they now appear:
keep me.

So that, God of unending patience and utter reliability,
to whom light and dark are as one,
I am held in you. Amen.

*Martyn Atkins, General Secretary and Secretary
of the British Methodist Conference*

19

Thirsty for you, O Christ, let us drink of the Living Water. Hungry for you, let us taste the Bread of Life. Longing for you, let us hear the Shepherd's voice. Amen.

*Anselm of Canterbury (c.1033-1109)*

**The Methodist Church in Southern Africa**

Presiding Bishop
Ziphozihle Siwa

**South Africa**

**Botswana**

**Lesotho**

**Mozambique**

Mission Partners
p/n  Malcolm Oliver and
Regina Siatwinda-
Oliver, Lyando and
Chipo

**Namibia**

**Swaziland**

Scholarship Students
Kasembele Massamba
Kameya Maina
Manyonga
(both in South Africa)

We give thanks for the growth of the Church in **Southern Africa**, evident in more churches being planted and an increase in new members;
for the encouraging journey of the new Seth Mokitimi Methodist Seminary under the leadership of its new President, the Revd Dr Mvume Dandala and his dedicated staff;
We pray that all members of the churches of Southern Africa may grow in discipleship, so that together they may become a healing community;
for the Church to continue to be a sign of God's presence in the world, working and praying for the "God of life to lead us to peace and justice";
for access to good quality education for all and the improvement of dysfunctional public education systems in the region.

*Ziphozihle Siwa, Presiding Bishop, Methodist Church of Southern Africa*

We pray today for those working in Josina Machel Island, **Mozambique** through partnership with MRDF. Give them the knowledge that their work is not only appreciated by those whom they are helping directly, but also by those in other countries who support their generous work through financial support and prayer.
May those who receive this invaluable help gain enough knowledge and confidence to be able to improve the production of food for sharing with everyone in their local communities, and relieve the hardships that they presently encounter in this area.
We pray that the problem of HIV/AIDS will be tackled with more input from other agencies in this area. Give all the people hope for the future, and the MRDF sufficient funding to continue your work in this region.

*Newbury Methodist Church, courtesy of MRDF*

We give thanks that the Methodist primary schools in the Bolton and Rochdale District play a key role in their communities;
for people of deep commitment and faith who care for their places of worship in practical and prayerful ways;
for churches working with refugees and asylum seekers, and those ministering to people adversely affected by the economic climate.
We pray that school chaplains, governors and staff would be aware of God's presence in times of challenge and change;
for ongoing conversations about the size and mission of circuits;
for the district as it works out its new mission statement in the light of the North West Review of Churches;
for greater shared ministry between presbyters and deacons.

**Bolton and
Rochdale District**

Chair
Paul Martin

---

**A prayer for the morning**
Generous God,
throughout this day,
lighten our tasks
and shine through our speaking.
May we reflect
your love in our lives,
your presence in our world,
and our trust and hope in you. Amen.

*(Paul Martin)*

**A prayer for the end of the day**
Eternal God,
when the light fails,
and the darkness enfolds us,
we look back on the day passed.
In celebrating the good things of this day
we also ask your forgiveness for our failings.
As you led your people with a fiery pillar,
lead us out of dark despair
into the light of your presence,
and the hope of a new and better tomorrow. Amen.

*Paul Martin, Bolton and Rochdale District Chair*

*(Bob Faraway)*

O Lord God, since you have called us to devote ourselves to the needs of others, grant us the strength of your grace. In the midst of our work let us not lose sight of your great purposes. Let us not snatch the management of your world from your hands, lest we faint and fall in the presence of your wisdom; this we beg for Jesu's sake. Amen.

*Florence Nightingale (1820-1910)*

### Zimbabwe

**Methodist Presiding Bishop**
Amos Ndhlumbi

**Mission Partners**
ed/sd Jonathan and Isobel Hill, Stephen and Susanna

### The United Church of Zambia

**General Secretary**
Peggy Mulambya Kabonde

**Mission Partners**
sd Jenny Featherstone [+CofS]
ed/m Keith and Ida Waddell, Mubita and Catriona [+CofS]
ed Glen and Wendy Lund, Julu, Kathleen, Taliesin and Tsunami

**Scholarship Students**
Chipasha Musaba (in Uganda)
Mwenifumbo Pona Hastings (in Britain)

Reconciling God, we pray for the people of **Zimbabwe** in another year of challenge. May the Church be a channel of your grace and unity in places of suspicion and division. We pray for the leaders and members of the Methodist Church, 'serving with courage'. Strengthen all who work at the Matthew Rusike Children's Home in Epworth and in outreach programmes throughout the nation, crossing social barriers to bring hope to families. We pray for political leaders, that justice and peace may accompany the political process. May the power and refreshment of your Holy Spirit flood the land, as the majesty of the Victoria Falls continually thunders to your glory.

*Jill Baker, Vice-President, Methodist Women in Britain*

We give thanks for the continued unity of the United Church of **Zambia** (UCZ) for over 50 years;
for the new UCZ leaders, elected last year;
for many years of peace which have allowed Zambia to host refugees fleeing from neighbouring war-torn countries.
We pray for Bishop Mutale Mulumbwa as he continues to lead the United Church of Zambia as Synod Bishop and for the Revd Peggy Mulambya Kabonde as she continues leading the UCZ as General Secretary;
for the resources to build a new office building for the UCZ;

for the Revd Rodwell Chomba newly elected as Bishop of Lusaka Presbytery.

*Richard Chimfwembe, Synod Mission and Evangelism Secretary, United Church of Zambia*

*Mutale Stannie Mulumbwa, Synod Bishop of the United Church of Zambia, was visibly moved when presented with a copy of Crossing the Chasm, the 2012/2013 Methodist Prayer Handbook (Steven Wild)*

We thank God for growing youth work in the Lakelands District, including residential youth camps 'Knekt' and 'No Limits' and collaboration with CEF, OM and YWAM; for coffee bar outreaches in Tempo and Sligo; for major regeneration of Pettigo town centre, including significant improvements to Pettigo Methodist Church paid for by the European Peace and Reconciliation Fund. We pray for ongoing healing and reconciliation following the 25th anniversary of the Enniskillen Remembrance Day bombing, and thank God for the progress made in 25 years.

**Lakelands (Ireland)**

Superintendent
Stephen Taylor

---

We give thanks for the support and welcome of the principal and staff at Trinity College, Bristol in providing a regular location for district meetings and activities; for workers with families and young people, including those at Badminton Road, Bristol; Chalford Hill; Chippenham; Clevedon; and Frampton Cotterell. We pray for the Midland Road Drop-in Centre in Bristol and its work among those who are too easily marginalised or forgotten, especially the ongoing review of its ways of working; for the outreach work of the Ark Bus in Bristol, a refitted double-decker bus, taking 'care and conversation' out to communities and challenging stereotypical views of Church; for Key Stage 2 project work for schools based at both the New Room and Charles Wesley's House.

**Bristol District**

Chair
Ward Jones

*Giving hope to the needy through food banks (Ward Jones)*

Lord, at times I struggle to be hopeful when I see
a world, with too many tragic headlines;
a Church trying to be faithful,
but uncertain about its future;
a neighbour rocked by bad news;
and I haven't even thought about myself, yet.

Hang on, though ... neither have I thought about you.
And I'd forgotten about when
I recognised your Spirit overflowing
in that aid project I heard about;
I shared in that unbelievably moving act of worship;
I heard about that broken relationship recently restored.
Wow! There is hope. I see light.
You are here alongside me. Amen.

*Ward Jones, Bristol District Chair*

23

*Let the fragrance of your glory draw us into your presence, O Christ.
Let the perfume of your love be our salvation and let the scent of your
sacrifice bring us your blessing. Amen.*

*Aelred of Rievaulx (c.1110-1167)*

**Kenya (Tanzania
and Uganda)**

**Methodist Presiding
Bishop**
Joseph Ntombura
 Mwaine

**Mission Partners**
n  Barbara Dickinson
d  Claire Smithson

**Scholarship Student**
Betty Nairuba
 (in Britain)

We give thanks for the support given by worldwide partners
for mission work in **Kenya** and for the dedicated ministers who
work in South Sudan, Congo and Tanzania with no stipend.
We pray for resources to allow training for all who wish to
become ministers.

*Stephen Kanyaru M'Impwii,
former Methodist Presiding Bishop, Kenya*

We thank God for the passion and dedication of the leaders in
the Methodist Church in Uganda.
We pray for ongoing plans to train, equip and encourage them,
and pray that the young, growing and mainly semi-urban and
rural congregations continue to be Christian mission frontiers
and life changers in the communities where they are planted.

*Eliab Amooti Bagambi, superintendent minister,
Methodist Church in Uganda.*

Lord, in the midst of conflicts, violence, doubt, despair, tensions
and fears, we pray that you may give the people of **Rwanda**
peace, faith, hope and justice.
We give thanks for the partnership between the Free Methodist
Church in Rwanda and the Wolverhampton and Shrewsbury
District and pray for the work they are doing together in order to
improve the lives of your people in Rwanda.

*Samuel Kayinamura, Bishop, Free Methodist Church in Rwanda*
*The Methodist Church in Rwanda
grew out of missionary work by the Free Methodist Church.
There are now over 250 Methodist churches across the country.*

*Rwandan women with
AIDS living in hope
(Susan Dutton)*

Loving God, we thank you for the signs of your transforming
presence in Rwanda. As we commemorate the end of the
genocide 20 years ago, we thank you for the many stories and
experiences we have witnessed of communities and churches
renewed by acts of Christian love and forgiveness. We thank
you for the commitment of both church and political leaders to
working for peace and reconciliation.

*Paul Nzacahayo, minister, Wolverhampton District*

We give thanks for Synod Cymru's place within the Methodist worldwide Connexion.

We pray for the new chair of Synod Cymru, Jennifer Hurd, that you will help her with the task of enabling the churches to bring light and hope to their communities, and to work ecumenically to strengthen the work and witness of the churches throughout Wales;

for the development of new police chaplaincy work in the Dyfed/Powys Constabulary, and to the farming communities;

that, even though local churches have few members, your light will shine brightly in their midst, giving them hope in their hearts which they can share in their communities.

**Yr Eglwys Fethodistaidd yng Nghymru**

**The Methodist Church in Wales**

**Y Cyngor (The Council)**

Synod Cymru Chair
Patrick Slattery

Wales Synod Chair
Jennifer Hurd

| | |
|---|---|
| Arglwydd pob goleuni | Lord of all light, |
| yn dy oleuni di y gwelwn oleuni, | in your light, we see light, |
| ac ynot ti nid oes dim tywyllch o gwbl. | and in you is no darkness at all. |
| Yn ein twywllch, dyro lewyrch ar ein llwybr ni; | In our darkness, bring light to our path; |
| yn ein dryswch, rho i ni obaith. | in our confusion, give us hope. |
| Boed i'th oleuni disgleirio trwyddom ni | May your light shine through us |
| i ddangos dy ffordd sy'n gariad. | to show your way that is love. |
| Er mwyn Iesu, | For the sake of Jesus, |
| goleuni'r byd. Amen. | the light of the world. Amen. |

*Jennifer Hurd, Wales Synod Chair*

We give thanks for the faithful commitment of staff and all the creative work which has been carried out by the Wales Training Network over many years;

for the continued work of the ecumenical chaplaincy team to Cardiff Bay based on the Cardiff Lightship and the development of an ecumenical chaplaincy team at the Royal Welsh Showground.

We pray for Jennifer Hurd as she returns to Wales to take up her new role as Chair/Cadeirydd of Synod Cymru, and for the Synod as they look to the future together;

for the work of Y Cyngor as it seeks to coordinate the response to the discussion papers arising from the Ecumenical Gathering at Aberystwyth last October;

for the staff who will form part of the new Discipleship and Ministries Learning Network serving the Methodist Church across Wales in both English and Welsh.

*Cardiff Bay lightship
(Stephen Wigley)*

Father of all, pour into our hearts the love that casts out fear, the truth that sets us free and the grace that is sufficient for all our needs, and grant that we may rejoice that though you are unseen, you are not unknown and that, though you are hidden from our eyes, we may behold your beauty at the last; through Christ our Lord. Amen.

*Louisa May Alcott (1832-1888)*

**Brazil**

Methodist Bishop
Adonias Pereira

**Uruguay**

Methodist President
Oscar Bolioli

**Argentina**

Methodist Bishop
Frank de Nully Brown

**Colombia**

Head of Church
Juan Alberto Cardona

**Venezuela**

President
Francisco Mendoza
Bracho

*Iguaçu Falls, between Brazil and Argentina (Thomas Quenet)*

We thank God for a generation of lay and ordained leaders in **Uruguay** that have been blazing a trail whose light has allowed the will of God to shine into the confusion and darkness of circumstance and history.
We pray for a new generation of lay and ordained workers who will renew mission during these new times.

*Oscar Bolioli, Methodist President, Uruguay*

We give thanks for the training of 50 lay ministers in the Evangelical Methodist Church in **Argentina**;
for the witness of the Church in Argentina in defending human rights, particularly the rights of indigenous people.
We pray for new disciples to join the local congregations.

*Frank de Nully Brown, Methodist Bishop, Argentina*

We give thanks for God's guidance in building the health clinic in the town of San Onofre, **Colombia**;
for having moved the hearts of Colombia's leaders, including those in both the government and the main guerilla group (FARC) to hold peace talks.
We pray for the new national coordinator of women's ministry that she may be able to maintain the passion and wisdom necessary to grow this ministry in every local church;
for the ministry among the indigenous Zenú people.

*Colombian Methodist Church*

Lord, we pray for the victims of natural disasters in Venezuela, that you would help them rebuild their shattered lives along with their homes and possessions. We pray that you would help those nations who emit high levels of carbon into the atmosphere to commit themselves seriously to reducing greenhouse emissions significantly.

*Francisco Mendoza Bracho, Methodist President, Venezuela*

*Hope is the first light of dawn unveiling the beauty of Lakeland.*
We give thanks for the Cumbria District's ministry to tourism.
We pray for all Christians making their discipleship real among the visitors to Cumbria's towns and rural centres.

*Hope is a new-born lamb struggling to its feet on frosted ground in the safety of its mother's care.*
We give thanks for Methodist chaplains in cattle markets across Cumbria.
We pray for farming communities facing a difficult year after consecutive wet seasons.

*Hope is the radiant smiles of a young couple making the down-payment on an affordable home.*
We give thanks for campaigns and schemes for affordable housing.
We pray for families who are being forced out of their own communities as the gap between poor and wealthy increases.

*Hope is the face of a child listening to story-time at Sure Start.*
We give thanks for the work of the 13 Action for Children Centres in Cumbria.
We pray for the planned new support centres for separated families.

*Hope is the relief on the face of a mother at a food bank.*
We give thanks for the growing response to the need for food banks in the district.
We pray for the increasing number of families living in poverty.

## Cumbria District

**Chair**
Richard Teal

*Wastwater
(Cumbria District)*

Dear Lord, we pray for the things we need to come quickly:
  to the hungry, food;
  to the weeping, joy;
  to the thirsty, water;
  to those living with war, peace;
  to those in poverty, a truly human life.
Give us patience to work for your kingdom.
Give us hope, that we may not weary in proclaiming it.
Give us vision to see your kingdom around us in the ordinary.
Give us light to see the horizon where your kingdom is fully known,
in Jesus Christ. Amen.

*Richard Teal, Cumbria District Chair*

Teach us, O Lord, the silent language of your presence, that we may adore you in the depths of our being and ask for nothing but knowledge of your will and the grace to accomplish it; through Christ our Lord. Amen.

*Jean Nicholas Grou (1731-1803)*

**Bolivia**

Methodist Bishop
Javier Rojas

**Chile**

Methodist Bishop
Mario Martinez

**Peru**

Methodist Bishop
Jorge Bravo-Caballero

**Ecuador**

Methodist Bishop
Silvio Cevallos

We give thanks for the support, encouragement and training given by the Methodist Church in **Chile** to women starting their own businesses in rural areas.
We pray for those who are suffering from exploitation or discrimination in an increasingly unequal society;
for those working to establish a centre to support young people and migrants from other parts of the region.

*Richard Vautrey, local preacher, Leeds*

We thank God for the relationship between the Methodist Church in Britain and the Methodist Church of **Peru**;
for the missionary work of pastors across Peru.
We pray for more mission workers to be called into the field;
for children and young adults in the Church in Peru;
for women who suffer all types of violence.

*Jorge Bravo-Caballero, Bishop, Methodist Church of Peru*

We thank God for new missions in the boroughs of Flavio Alfaro, Chone and Calceta in the Manabi province of **Ecuador**;
for mission initiatives in the city of Quevedo in the Laguna area;
for the boroughs of Cayambe in the El Prado area and for the English language mission initiative in the city of Cuenca that began in February 2013.
We pray that the Lord will continue to bless these initiatives and meet their every need so that the mission may continue to grow for the glory and praise of his holy name.

*Methodist Church in Ecuador*

*A small church near Pichihue, Chile (Richard Vautrey)*

**Benediction**
May the loving God embrace us;
may the healing Christ restore us;
may the powerful Spirit encourage us;
may God, the three in one, go with us. Amen.

*Colin Bemrose, worship leader, Rugby*

We give thanks that Derry/Londonderry is City of Culture 2013; for youth and children's work in the North West District, especially in Dunkineely and in Togherdoo.
We pray for circuits dealing with major changes due to staffing difficulties;
for hospital, university and prison chaplains in Coleraine, Magilligan, Londonderry, Letterkenny and Omagh;
for the north-west part of Co Donegal where a monthly act of witness takes place in a small 'Café Church' gathering in Letterkenny.

**North West District (Ireland)**

Superintendent
John Sweeney

We give thanks for the impact of Messy Church across the Channel Islands District. We celebrate the faith and commitment of the community at Philadelphie who have decided to cease worship in their building on a Sunday, so that it can be reshaped for use as a Messy Church centre during the week;
for the opportunities for pastoral conversations given by the screening of the BBC's *An Island Parish* series based on Sark;
for the visit of almost 30 Brazilian Methodists to Guernsey to lead 'Encounter with God' weekends, and for the growing links between Channel Island and Brazilian Methodism.
We pray for the continuing development of town-centre ministry in St Helier, and for the new Paradise Community Café opened in the St Helier Methodist Centre;
for the creation of a half-time MHA chaplaincy appointment to serve in Maison L'Aumone Care Home, and Maison de Quetteville Dementia Care Home in Guernsey.

**Channel Islands District**

Chair
David Hinchliffe

O God of land and sea and air,
we thank you for the beauty of the Channel Islands,
from the rising of the sun, to its setting over the sea,
we pray for the crews of the lifeboats,
the Channel Islands Air Search, and
the Flying Christine sea ambulance
who risk their lives in the service of those in need
in the islands and waters of the Channel Islands District,
and who bring light and hope
to those in great danger.
May the God of hope go with them every day. Amen.

*David Hinchliffe, Channel Island District Chair*

*The blessing of the fleet, Sea Sunday, Guernsey (Kathryn Hinchliffe)*

## Praying with Christians in Latin America

Holy God, too great to be trifled with and too wise to be deceived by insincerity; compose our thoughts as we enter your presence, order our minds as we bring our petitions, and grant us grace to offer you the loving sacrifice of hearts both steadfast and obedient; through Jesus Christ our Lord. Amen.

*Susanna Wesley (1669-1742)*

**Methodist Church in the Caribbean and the Americas (MCCA)**

Connexional President
Otto Wade

**Leeward Islands District (MCCA)**

District President
Franklyn Manners

**Guyana District (MCCA)**

District President
Glenna Spencer

Mission Partners
p/ed Mark° and
    Carolyn Lawrence

**Panama/Costa Rica District (MCCA)**

District President
Heinsley Johnson

We give thanks for the new computer lab at the Gilbert Agricultural and Rural Development centre; for the opportunities given to the beneficiaries of the East Caribbean Youth Microenterprise Programme. We pray for the development of **Antigua** and **Barbuda** at a time when the tourism industry is floundering.

*Christopher and Vera Lacey, former mission partners,*
*Antigua, Leeward Islands District, MCCA*

Gracious God we thank you for the resilience, perseverance and hospitality of the people of **Guyana**, even in the face of difficulties.
We pray for the work in schools and ask that your light may shine in the lives of those children who do not yet know you; for the outreach to the men in Guyana, that husbands and fathers may find their hope in Jesus and have the courage to lead their families in God's ways.

*Carolyn Lawrence, mission partner, Guyana District, MCCA*

Almighty God, as the waters flow from the Chirripo mountain to the vast ocean, so your mercies roll down to every child of God in Panama.
We thank you for the for the ongoing witness of the Church in the Valiente Peninsula, preparing for its centenary in 2017; for the new ventures of the high school in Colon; for the progress of the work in the Bocas del Toro Circuit.
We come to you with the energy of Volcán Barú to pray for the **Panama/Costa Rica** District which faces economic hardship, unemployment, underemployment, social and moral decay, family disintegration, proliferation of crime and violence, disregard for the sanctity of human life, and disrespect for authority.

*Heinsley Johnson, Panama/Costa Rica District President*

We give thanks for the ministry of street pastors, phone link services, food banks, family support services, credit unions, coffee bars and cafés across the Chester and Stoke-on-Trent District which are bringing light and hope to people in tough times;
for the Beacon House of Prayer, which is drawing people across the city of Stoke-in-Trent to pray for their communities, their city, the nation and the world;
for the Churches Together in Cheshire Agricultural Chaplaincy which offers hope to communities and individuals in rural Cheshire and beyond;
We pray for one another that we may "shine like stars"* in our places of work, communities, and homes;
for Saltbox which seeks to be salt and light in every aspect of civic life in the city of Stoke.
for the work of chaplaincy to the Chamber of Commerce and businesses and the traditional chaplaincies to hospitals, prisons and residential facilities.

### Chester and Stoke-on-Trent District

Chair
Peter Barber

*A young boy in Ethiopia is light and hope to his grandmother (Peter Barber)*

Gracious God,
      where there is confusion, bring the light of understanding;
      where there is pain, bring the light of loving care;
      where there is fear, bring the light of comfort;
      where there is hurt and division, bring the light of forgiveness;
      where there are endings, bring the hope of new beginning;
      where there is sadness and regret, bring the hope of fresh possibilities;
      where there is brokenness, bring the hope of reconciliation;
      where there is death, bring the hope of resurrection;
for you are our light and our hope. Amen.
*Peter Barber, Chester and Stoke-on-Trent District Chair*

### A prayer for those in public office

We pray for everyone in involved in public life;
for councillors and mayors, the government and MPs;
that those who seek power will be driven by a vocation to serve,
that they will set a high value on integrity and honesty,
in matters of finance and of speaking the truth,
and that they will exercise the authority vested in them,
with imagination, intelligence, wisdom and compassion. Amen.
*Jenny Dyer, superintendent, Derby Circuit*

*(Philippians 2:15)

31

Jesus, abject and despised, let us not be ashamed to follow you. Jesus, hated and persecuted, let us not be afraid to walk in your footsteps. Jesus, blasphemed and condemned, let us be counted your friends. Jesus, mocked and scourged, let us bear all things patiently. Jesus, crowned and derided, let us not be overwhelmed by our injuries and grief. Amen.

*John Wesley (1703-1791)*

**Belize/Honduras District (MCCA)**

District President
Roosevelt Papouloute

Mission Partners
p/sd Andrew° and
Julie Cunningham,
Elijah and Hannah

**South Caribbean District (MCCA)**

District President
Cuthbert Edwards

Mission Partner
ed Andrew Dye

**Bahamas/Turks and Caicos Islands District (MCCA)**

District President
Derek Browne

We give thanks for the beauty of the **Turks and Caicos Islands** which attract tourists, thus providing work for local people; that no lives were lost in Hurricane Sandy in the autumn of 2012;
that the **Bahamas** celebrate the 40th anniversary of their independence in 2013.
We pray for the new governments of both Turks and Caicos and Bahamas which were elected during 2012;
for the victims of crime and violence as the murder rate continues to increase;
for those living with HIV/AIDS and those who support them and care for them.

*Eddie Sykes, former mission partner,*
*Bahamas/Turks and Caicos Islands District, MCCA*

We give thanks for **Grenada**'s fertile soil which means food crops grow all year round, energised by the Caribbean sunlight; for the hard work and care of teachers who seek to bring light as they teach in difficult conditions and with few resources; for the work that God is doing through the Church to bring hope to young people.
We pray for the young men who hang around 'liming' on street corners, smoking and drinking rum;
for those who face domestic abuse and for those who seek to bring hope and support;
that the Churches will be united and work together, rather than focusing on denominational disputes.

*Andrew Dye, mission partner, Grenada,*
*South Caribbean District, MCCA*

*20 year-old Renaldo Gibson was severely injured in a car accident in 2009 and not given any hope of recovery. He is always smiling, always trusting, despite his challenges. (Eddie Sykes)*

Almighty God, kindle in us the fire of your love, and help every Christian disciple in Cornwall to become a burning and shining light, bringing hope to all people.
Hope – for the new children and families worker in the Callington and Gunnislake Circuit and her excellent new initiatives including the 'Pop Up' youth choir.
Light – in the 80 people who enrolled on the six week Holy Spirit course at Chapel St Church Penzance.
Hope – in the proliferation of Messy Church ventures across the district.
Light – in the people committed to being Street Pastors in Camborne, Falmouth, Truro, St Austell and Newquay.

*Steven Wild, Cornwall District Chair*

## Cornwall District

**Chair**
Steven Wild

*Rainbow of hope in St Ives, Cornwall (Steven Wild)*

Lord Jesus, our hope is in you.
Help us to develop ecumenical relationships in our circuits so that we may be united in our work for you.
Help us to see the way forward for the common good of all people.
May your hope for the world come alive through us.
Strengthen us, for your hope is in us. Amen.

*Ruth Braddock, Truro Circuit*

**Prayer for Methodist Homes (MHA)**
God of love and hope, of encouragement and challenge, in MHA's 70th anniversary year we offer thanks for the ways MHA has given love and Christian service among the oldest in our communities.
As we look to the future, we pray for the work of MHA:
for those who live in the MHA homes and schemes;
for those who care for them;
for those whose vision enables new ways of caring;
for those in the organisation who direct and manage;
for those who support this work with prayer and fundraising.
We acknowledge our need of one another
and ask for your gifts of wisdom and understanding,
that the love of Christ may be shown in all we do. Amen.

*Margaret Goodall, Chaplaincy Adviser, Methodist Homes*

Give the gift of friendship
**MHA**
Celebrating 70 Years of Care

O Christ of the dove, grant us the purity of the Spirit. O Christ of the sparrow, grant us the Father's protection. O Christ of the mother-hen, grant us shelter beneath your wing. Amen.

*Bonaventure of Bagnoregio (1221-1274)*

### Jamaica District (MCCA)

**District President**
Everald Galbraith

**Scholarship Student**
Phillip Robinson°
(in Jamaica)

### Haiti District (MCCA)

**District President**
Gesner Paul

**Mission Partners**
d/ed  John and Sharon
Harbottle

### Cuba

**Methodist Bishop**
Ricardo Pereira Díaz

### The Evangelical Church in the Dominican Republic

**Head of Church**
Miguel Angel Cancú

### Guatemala

**Methodist Bishop**
Tomas Riquiac Ixtan

### Puerto Rico

**Methodist Bishop**
Rafael Moreno Rivas

*Sowing seeds of hope: Adrian Williams and Leroy Campbell plant trees for the 250th anniversary of Methodism in the MCCA (Everald Galbraith)*

We thank God for the dedication of the local preachers, the backbone of the preaching ministry in the **Jamaica District**;
for the new Confirmation class manual and catechism.
We pray for the Jamaican Government as efforts are made to reduce the indebtedness of the country and as negotiations for an agreement with the International Monetary Fund continue;
for the success of the child protection initiative, Operation SAVE 50.
*Everald Galbraith, President, Jamaica District, MCCA*

*Papa letenal* (Eternal Father),
we pray for the country of **Haiti** which is so exposed to the forces of nature and where disaster has struck many times. Thank you for those whom you have called to serve you as mission partners there. Work through them, we ask, to bring healing to the sick, and the message of your love in all that they do. Protect them, and the people of Haiti, particularly in the hours of darkness and in the depths of despair. *An kabab sou nou epi rete tout tan avek nou*. Amen.

* Creole: blessing be with us now and always. Amen.
*Hilary Cheng, minister, Cambridge Circuit*

Lord God, we pray that you will bring hope and encouragement to all those working the land in **Guatemala**;
that everyone will grow in knowledge and practical skills and pass these on to future generations to enable the Mayan community to achieve self-sufficiency through a productive and sustainable farming culture. Amen.
*Newbury Methodist Church, courtesy of MRDF*

We give thanks for the continued blessing of God on work and outreach across the North East District through ministry in both urban and rural communities;
for the continued growth of the first joint Methodist/Anglican Church in Ireland, the Church of the Good Shepherd in Monkstown, Newtownabbey, which stands out as a beacon of unity in a very divided land;
for the continued work of peace-making and bridge-building between divided communities in Ireland.
We pray for wisdom for the student chaplain at the University of Ulster in Jordanstown;
for the end of conflict on the streets of the district.

**North East District (Ireland)**

Superintendent
Aian Ferguson

---

We give thanks for those committed to sharing the light and hope of the gospel with women, men and children who find themselves in dark and despairing places;
for chaplains in hospitals, schools, prisons, industry, commerce and rural areas, who draw alongside others and help them to glimpse God walking with them;
for all people who respond to God's call and embrace the joys and challenges of being a disciple of Jesus.
We pray for the new initiatives in mission in Catterick Garrison, Durham, Thornaby and many other places in the district;
for our ecumenical partners and for increased understanding and cooperation in all areas of our life together;
for all those serving in local government as the region faces increasing economic and social challenges.

**Darlington District**

Chair
Ruth Gee

Jesus, light of the world:
  in the darkness of anxiety be the glimmer of peace;
  in the darkness of sorrow be the glimmer of joy;
  in the darkness of suffering be the glimmer of comfort;
  in the darkness of rejection be the glimmer of welcome;
  in the darkness of despair be the glimmer of hope.
So may the light that cannot be overcome
  shine through the darkness,
  shine through our lives,
  shine in the world. Amen.
          *Ruth Gee, Darlington District Chair and*
*President of the British Methodist Conference, 2013/2014*

*Jesus, light of the world*
*(photo: Val Facey)*

Lord, before ever you made us, you loved us. Nor has your love ever slackened, nor ever shall. In love all your works have begun, and in love they continue. In this love our life is everlasting, and in this love we shall see you and be glad forever. Amen.

*Julian of Norwich (1342-1416)*

**United Methodist Church (USA)**

Ecumenical Officer to the Council of Bishops
Mary Ann Swenson

**The United Church of Canada**

General Secretary
Nora Sanders

**Mexico**

Methodist Bishop
Raúl Garcia de Ochoa

**The Methodist Church in El Salvador**

Methodist President
Juan De Dios Peña

Mission Partners
ed/ed  Paul Collins and
   Maura Cook, Scout,
   Assisi and Saffi

**Nicaragua**

Methodist Bishop
Eduardo Rodriguez

Almighty Creator, our thoughts turn to our brothers and sisters serving and working in the United Methodist Church in the **USA**. We ask for hope in their disappointments and we pray that they may know the spirit of revival and enthusiasm that will make an impact on the faith of the people. We pray that you will guide and direct them to continue in their endeavours, that the word of God may flourish in the hearts and minds of those it reaches. Bless your people in the USA, Lord, and fill them with desire to continue the work of the kingdom.

*Lori Broschat, Dakotas Annual Conference,*
*United Methodist Church*

We give thanks for all the people, including the staff of the General Council Office, who work to foster healthy, sustainable church ministries in the United Church of **Canada** (UCC).
As the UCC becomes an intercultural and multilingual Church we pray for new insights for her members on how to celebrate God's presence in this changing reality;
for a United Church that is grounded in Jesus Christ, and alive with justice, diversity, and spiritual vitality.

*Alydia Smith, Programme Coordinator, Worship, Music and*
*Spirituality, United Church of Canada*

We pray for God's blessing on those who are working with the communities displaced by civil war in **El Salvador**;
for the farmers of El Salvador whose livelihoods have been affected by erratic weather and deforestation;
for God's blessing on those who have been helping them to introduce sustainable farming techniques and have given the farmers security for the present, and a future for their country.

*Newbury Methodist Church, courtesy of MRDF*

# Lectionary Readings and Psalms

This table of readings, hymns and psalms (Ps) has been prepared by Norman Wallwork. Major holy days and special days of prayer and observation have been included.

For a daily reflection and commentary on the readings visit *A Word in Time* www.methodistchurch.org.uk/bible

Ps = Psalm
StF = *Singing the Faith*

# A guide to daily prayer

Printed below is one possible way of making use of *Singing the Faith* as a daily prayer companion linked with the material provided each day in the Prayer Handbook and in the centre fold of Lectionary Readings and Psalms.

*O Lord, open our lips,*
*and we shall praise your name.*

Hymn – from the Lectionary

Psalm – from the Lectionary

Reading – from the Lectionary

Canticle – from *Singing the Faith*

| | | |
|---|---|---|
| Sunday | 796 | A Song of Resurrection |
| | or 799 | *Te Deum Laudamus* |
| Monday | 792 | *Benedictus* – The Song of Zechariah |
| Tuesday | 798 | Great and Wonderful |
| Wednesday | 791 | A Song of Creation |
| Thursday | 797 | A Song of Christ's Glory |
| Friday | 795 | Saviour of the World |
| Saturday | 793 | *Magnificat* – The Song of Mary |
| | or 794 | *Nunc Dimittis* – The Song of Simeon |

Prayer of the Day – from the top left hand box of the page for the day

Intercession and Reflection – from the appropriate day of the Handbook
or from the opening pages of the Handbook

The Lord's Prayer

The Grace

Week beginning 25 August
21st in Ordinary Time
**Songs of Salvation**

| | | | |
|---|---|---|---|
| S 25 | Luke 13:10-17 | StF416 | Ps 103:1-8 |
| M26 | Revelation 15:2-4 | StF94 | Ps 105 |
| T 27 | Revelation 19:1-8 | StF753 | Ps 106 |
| W28 | Revelation 21:1-7 | StF224 | Ps 107 |
| T 29bc | Matthew 14:1-12 | StF732 | Ps 11 |
| F 30 | Revelation 21:22-27 | StF94 | Ps 115 |
| S 31 | Revelation 22:1-5 | StF593 | Ps 121 |

[bc=Beheading of John the Baptist]

Week beginning 1 September
22nd in Ordinary Time
**The New Israel**

| | | | |
|---|---|---|---|
| S 1 | Luke 14:1, 7-14 | StF362 | Ps 112 |
| M2 | Joshua 1:1-11 | StF473 | Ps 1 |
| T 3 | Joshua 2:1-24 | StF313 | Ps 2 |
| W4 | Joshua 3:1-17 | StF465 | Ps 3 |
| T 5 | Joshua 4:1–5:1 | StF470 | Ps 4 |
| F 6 | Joshua 5:13–6:20 | StF459 | Ps 5 |
| S 7 | Joshua 7:1-15 | StF346 | Ps 6:1-9 |

Week beginning 8 September
23rd in Ordinary Time
**The Covenant God**

| | | | |
|---|---|---|---|
| S 8a | Luke 14:25-33 | StF563 | |
| | | | Ps 139:1-6, 13-18 |
| M 9b | Luke 1:39-47 | StF482 | Ps 45 |
| T 10 | Joshua 7:16-26 | StF455 | Ps 7:1-11 |
| W11 | Joshua 8:10-29 | StF457 | Ps 8 |
| T 12 | Joshua 9:3-27 | StF459 | Ps 9:1-10 |
| F 13 | Joshua 24:1-28 | StF645 | Ps 10:1-12 |
| S 14c | Philippians 2:5-11 | StF279 | Ps 22 |

[a=Racial Justice Sunday; b=Nativity of Virgin Mary trans.; c=Holy Cross Day]

Week beginning 15 September
24th in Ordinary Time
**God's Chosen Leader**

| | | | |
|---|---|---|---|
| S 15 | Luke 15:1-10 | StF323 | Ps 51 |
| M16 | Matthew 1:18-25 | StF178 | Ps 11:1-5 |
| T 17 | Matthew 2:1-12 | StF222 | Ps 12 |
| W18 | Matthew 2:13-23 | StF218 | Ps 13 |
| T 19 | Matthew 3:1-17 | StF233 | Ps 15 |
| F 20 | Matthew 4:1-22 | StF247 | Ps 16 |
| S 21d | Matthew 9:9-13 | StF454 | Ps 49 |

[d=Matthew, Apostle and Evangelist]

Week beginning 22 September
25th in Ordinary Time
**Living in God's Way**

| | | | |
|---|---|---|---|
| S 22 | Luke 16:1-13 | StF563 | Ps 113 |
| M23 | Matthew 4:23–5:12 | StF245 | Ps 17 |
| T 24 | Matthew 5:13-20 | StF255 | Ps 18:1-16 |
| W25 | Matthew 5:21-26 | StF691 | Ps 19 |
| T 26 | Matthew 5:27-37 | StF566 | Ps 20 |
| F 27 | Matthew 5:38-48 | StF276 | Ps 21:1-7 |
| S 28 | Matthew 6:1-18 | StF522 | Ps 23 |

Week beginning 29 September
26th in Ordinary Time
**The Life of Prayer**

| | | | |
|---|---|---|---|
| S 29 | Luke 16:19-31 | StF80 | Ps 146 |
| M30e | John 1:47-51 | StF91 | Ps 69 |
| T 1 | Matthew 6:19-34 | StF748 | Ps 22:1-21 |
| W2 | Matthew 7:1-28 | StF705 | Ps 22:22-31 |
| T 3 | Matthew 8:1-13 | StF685 | Ps 24 |
| F 4 | Matthew 8:14-22 | StF421 | Ps 25 |
| S 5 | Matthew 8:23–9:1 | StF241 | Ps 26 |

[e=Michael and All Angels, trans.]

Week beginning 6 October
27th in Ordinary Time
**The Bridegroom's Guests**

| | | | |
|---|---|---|---|
| S 6 | Luke 17:5-10 | StF509 | Ps 37:1-9 |
| M7 | Matthew 9:2-13 | StF250 | Ps 27 |
| T 8 | Matthew 9:14-26 | StF650 | Ps 29 |
| W9 | Matthew 9:27-38 | StF503 | Ps 30 |
| T 10 | Matthew 10:1-15 | StF404 | Ps 31:1-8 |
| F 11 | Matthew 10:16-33 | StF745 | Ps 31:9-24 |
| S 12 | Matthew 10:34–11:1 | StF222 | Ps 32 |

Week beginning 13 October
28th in Ordinary Time
**The Forerunner**

| | | | |
|---|---|---|---|
| S 13 | Luke 17:11-19 | StF653 | Ps 111 |
| M14 | Matthew 11:2-19 | StF164 | Ps 33 |
| T 15 | Matthew 11:20-30 | StF328 | Ps 34:1-10 |
| W16 | Matthew 12:1-21 | StF591 | Ps 34:11-22 |
| T 17 | Matthew 12:22-37 | StF408 | Ps 35:9-18 |
| F 18f | 2 Timothy 4:5-17 | StF664 | Ps 145 |
| S 19 | Matthew 12:38-50 | StF255 | Ps 36 |

[f=Luke the Evangelist]

Week beginning 20 October
29th in Ordinary Time
## The Voice of Wisdom

| | | | |
|---|---|---|---|
| S 20 | Luke 18:1-8 | StF529 | Ps 121 |
| M21 | Proverbs 1:20-33 | StF623 | Ps 37:1-11 |
| T 22 | Proverbs 2:1-15 | StF450 | Ps 37:12-29 |
| W23 | Proverbs 3:1-26 | StF444 | Ps 37:30-40 |
| T 24 | Proverbs 4:1-18 | StF562 | Ps 38:1-9 |
| F 25 | Proverbs 6:1-19 | StF507 | Ps 38:10-22 |
| S 26 | Proverbs 8:1-21 | StF500 | Ps 39 |

[One World Week]

Week beginning 27 October
30th in Ordinary Time
## Firm Foundations

| | | | |
|---|---|---|---|
| S 27 | Luke 18:9-14 | StF34 | Ps 84 |
| M28g | John 15:17-27 | StF677 | Ps 117 |
| T 29 | Proverbs 8:22-36 | StF247 | Ps 40:1-10 |
| W30 | Proverbs 9:1-18 | StF501 | Ps 41 |
| T 31 | Proverbs 10:1-13 | StF79 | Ps 42 |
| F 1h | Luke 6:20-31 | StF746 | Ps 149 |
| S 2 | Proverbs 11:1-12 | StF703 | Ps 43 |

[g=Simon and Jude, Apostles; h=All Saints' Day]

Week beginning 3 November
31st in Ordinary Time
## The Way of the Righteous

| | | | |
|---|---|---|---|
| S 3i | Matthew 5:1-12 | StF744 | Ps 148 |
| M4 | Proverbs 12:10-22 | StF506 | Ps 44:1-8 |
| T 5 | Proverbs 14:31–15:8 | StF693 | Ps 45 |
| W6 | Proverbs 15:18-33 | StF238 | Ps 46 |
| T 7 | Proverbs 20:1-9 | StF498 | Ps 47 |
| F 8 | Proverbs 22:1-9 | StF123 | Ps 48 |
| S 9 | Proverbs 31:10-20 | StF608 | Ps 49 |

[i=All Saints' Sunday]

Week beginning 10 November
32nd in Ordinary Time
## Words and Actions

| | | | |
|---|---|---|---|
| S 10j | Luke 20:27-38 | StF348 | Ps 17:1-9 |
| M11 | James 1:1-11 | StF180 | Ps 50:1-15 |
| T 12 | James 1:12-18 | StF456 | Ps 51 |
| W13 | James 1:19-27 | StF668 | Ps 52 |
| T 14 | James 2:1-7 | StF654 | Ps 53 |
| F 15 | James 2:8-26 | StF249 | Ps 54 |
| S 16 | James 3:1-12 | StF93 | Ps 56 |

[j=Remembrance Sunday]

Week beginning 17 November
33rd in Ordinary Time
## Prayer and Faith

| | | | |
|---|---|---|---|
| S 17 | Luke 21:5-19 | StF696 | Ps 98 |
| M18 | James 3:13-18 | StF334 | Ps 55:1-8 |
| T 19 | James 4:1-12 | StF681 | Ps 55:16-22 |
| W20 | James 4:13-17 | StF611 | Ps 57 |
| T 21 | James 5:1-6 | StF732 | Ps 61 |
| F 22 | James 5:7-12 | StF503 | Ps 62 |
| S 23 | James 5:13-19 | StF518 | Ps 63:1-8 |

[Prisons Week]

Week beginning 24 November
Week before Advent
## King of Kings

| | | | |
|---|---|---|---|
| S 24kl | Luke 23:33-43 | StF284 | Ps 46 |
| M25 | Isaiah 40:1-11 | StF183 | Ps 8 |
| T 26 | Isaiah 40:12-26 | StF705 | Ps 110 |
| W27 | Isaiah 40:27–41:7 | StF89 | Ps 145 |
| T 28 | Isaiah 41:8-20 | StF87 | Ps 2 |
| F 29 | Isaiah 41:21-29 | StF172 | Ps 5 |
| S 30m | Matthew 4:18-22 | StF250 | Ps 28 |

[k=Christ the King; l=Women Against Violence
Sunday; m=Andrew, Apostle]

Week beginning 1 December
1st of Advent
## The Lord's Servant

| | | | |
|---|---|---|---|
| S 1n | Matthew 24:36-44 | StF780 | Ps 122 |
| M2 | Isaiah 42:1-17 | StF228 | Ps 64 |
| T 3 | Isaiah 42:18-25 | StF511 | Ps 65 |
| W4 | Isaiah 43:1-13 | StF455 | Ps 66 |
| T 5 | Isaiah 43:14-28 | StF470 | Ps 67 |
| F 6 | Isaiah 44:1-8 | StF157 | Ps 68:1-20 |
| S 7 | Isaiah 44:9-23 | StF470 | Ps 68:24-32 |

[n=World AIDS Day]

Week beginning 8 December
2nd of Advent
## The Unfolding Purpose

| | | | |
|---|---|---|---|
| S 8 | Matthew 3:1-12 | StF182 | Ps 85 |
| M9 | Isaiah 44:24-28 | StF298 | Ps 69:1-21 |
| T 10 | Isaiah 45:1-13 | StF536 | Ps 69:29-36 |
| W11 | Isaiah 45:14-25 | StF19 | Ps 71:1-14 |
| T 12 | Isaiah 46:1-13 | StF502 | Ps 71:15-24 |
| F 13 | Isaiah 47:1-15 | StF338 | Ps 73:1-14 |
| S 14 | Isaiah 48:1-11 | StF508 | Ps 73:15-24 |

## Week beginning 15 December
3rd of Advent
### Faithful and Waiting

| | | | |
|---|---|---|---|
| S 15 | Matthew 11:2-11 | StF164 | Ps 146 |
| M16 | Isaiah 48:12-22 | StF338 | Ps 30 |
| T 17 | Isaiah 50:4-10 | StF319 | Ps 72:1-11 |
| W18 | Isaiah 54:1-10 | StF66 | Ps 72:12-20 |
| T 19 | Luke 1:5-25 | StF188 | Ps 76 |
| F 20 | Luke 1:26-38 | StF187 | Ps 24 |
| S 21 | Luke 1:39-45 | StF196 | Ps 2 |

## Week beginning 22 December
4th of Advent and Christmas
### Manger and Cross

| | | | |
|---|---|---|---|
| S 22 | Matthew 1:18-25 | StF178 | Ps 80 |
| M23 | Malachi 3:1-4 | StF508 | Ps 25 |
| T 24 | Luke 1:67-79 | StF169 | Ps 89:1-18 |
| W25o | Luke 2:1-20 | StF195 | Ps 110 |
| T 26p | Acts 7:51-60 | StF188 | Ps 13 |
| F 27q | 1 John 2:3-11 | StF366 | Ps 117 |
| S 28r | Jeremiah 31:15-17 | StF218 | Ps 124 |

[o=Christmas Day; p=Stephen, Martyr;
q=John, Evangelist; r=Holy Innocents]

## Week beginning 29 December
1st of Christmas
### Truth and Freedom

| | | | |
|---|---|---|---|
| S 29 | Matthew 2:13-23 | StF218 | Ps 148 |
| M30 | 1 John 2:12-17 | StF370 | Ps 96:1-9 |
| T 31 | 1 John 2:18-21 | StF338 | Ps 96:10-13 |
| W1s | Luke 2:15-21 | StF354 | Ps 8 |
| T 2 | 1 John 2:22-28 | StF636 | Ps 98:1-3 |
| F 3 | 1 John 2:29–3:6 | StF82 | Ps 98:4-9 |
| S 4 | 1 John 3:7-10 | StF548 | Ps 97 |

[s=Naming and Circumcision of Jesus]

## Week beginning 5 January
2nd of Christmas
### The True Light

| | | | |
|---|---|---|---|
| S 5t | John 1:1-18 | StF202 | Ps 147 |
| M6u | Matthew 2:1-12 | StF228 | Ps 72 |
| T 7 | 1 John 3:11-21 | StF686 | Ps 146 |
| W8 | 1 John 4:7-10 | StF742 | Ps 147 |
| T 9 | 1 John 4:11-16 | StF620 | Ps 148 |
| F 10 | 1 John 4:17-21 | StF125 | Ps 149 |
| S 11 | 1 John 5:1-21 | StF503 | Ps 150 |

[t=Epiphany Sunday & Covenant Sunday;
u=Epiphany]

## Week beginning 12 January
1st in Ordinary Time
### Call to Repentance

| | | | |
|---|---|---|---|
| S 12v | Matthew 3:13-17 | StF233 | Ps 29 |
| M13 | Joel 1:1-14 | StF561 | Ps 99 |
| T 14 | Joel 1:15-20 | StF741 | Ps 100 |
| W15 | Joel 2:1-17 | StF64 | Ps 102:1-11 |
| T 16 | Joel 2:18-27 | StF94 | Ps 102:12-28 |
| F 17 | Joel 2:28-32 | StF370 | Ps 103 |
| S 18w | Joel 3:1-16 | StF190 | Ps 105:1-15 |

[v=Baptism of Christ; w=Octave of Prayer for
Christian Unity begins]

## Week beginning 19 January
2nd in Ordinary Time
### Unity in Christ

| | | | |
|---|---|---|---|
| S 19 | John 1:29-42 | StF347 | Ps 40 |
| M20 | Jeremiah 33:6-9a | StF355 | Ps 104:1-23 |
| T 21 | Ephesians 4:1-6 | StF690 | Ps 104:24-35 |
| W22 | John 17:11b-23 | StF675 | Ps 107:1-16 |
| T 23 | Ezekiel 37:15-23 | StF185 | Ps 107:17-32 |
| F 24 | 1 Corinthians 12:1-11 | StF661 | Ps 107:33-43 |
| S 25x | Galatians 1:11-24 | StF450 | Ps 139 |

[x=Conversion of Paul, Apostle]

## Week beginning 26 January
3rd in Ordinary Time
### The Gospel of God

| | | | |
|---|---|---|---|
| S 26 | Matthew 4:12-23 | StF674 | Ps 27 |
| M27y | Romans 1:1-7 | StF9 | Ps 106:1-8 |
| T 28 | Romans 1:8-17 | StF320 | Ps 106:43-48 |
| W29 | Romans 1:18-32 | StF118 | Ps 110 |
| T 30 | Romans 2:1-16 | StF717 | Ps 111 |
| F 31 | Romans 2:17-29 | StF732 | Ps 112 |
| S 1 | Romans 3:1-20 | StF336 | Ps 113 |

[Poverty & Homelessness Action Week;
y=Holocaust Memorial Day]

## Week beginning 2 February
4th in Ordinary Time
### Justified by Faith

| | | | |
|---|---|---|---|
| S 2z | Luke 2:22-32 | StF232 | Ps 24 |
| M3 | Romans 3:21-31 | StF322 | Ps 114 |
| T 4 | Romans 4:1-12 | StF458 | Ps 115 |
| W5 | Romans 4:13-25 | StF304 | Ps 116 |
| T 6 | Romans 5:1-11 | StF286 | Ps 117 |
| F 7 | Romans 5:12-21 | StF63 | Ps 118:1-18 |
| S 8 | Romans 6:1-14 | StF775 | Ps 118:19-29 |

[z=7Sunday of the Presentation of Christ in the
Temple, Candlemas]

Week beginning 9 February
5th in Ordinary Time
**Grace Abounding**

| | | | |
|---|---|---|---|
| S 9 | Matthew 5:13-20 | StF255 | Ps 112 |
| M10 | Romans 6:15-23 | StF566 | Ps 23 |
| T 11 | Romans 7:1-6 | StF326 | Ps 25 |
| W12 | Romans 7:7-25 | StF436 | Ps 26 |
| T 13 | Romans 8:1-11 | StF149 | Ps 27 |
| F 14 | Romans 8:12-17 | StF548 | Ps 29 |
| S 15 | Romans 8:18-30 | StF727 | Ps 30 |

Week beginning 16 February
6th in Ordinary Time
**God's Love in Christ**

| | | | |
|---|---|---|---|
| S 16aa | Matthew 5:21-37 | StF691 | Ps 119:1-8 |
| M17 | Romans 8:31-39 | StF561 | Ps 119:9-16 |
| T 18 | Romans 9:1-13 | StF91 | Ps 119:17-32 |
| W19 | Romans 9:14-29 | StF516 | Ps 119:49-64 |
| T 20 | Romans 9:30–10:10 | StF416 | Ps 119:65-80 |
| F 21 | Romans 10:11-21 | StF418 | Ps 119:81-96 |
| S 22 | Romans 11:1-12 | StF3 | Ps 119:97-112 |

[aa=Education Sunday]

Week beginning 23 February
6th in Ordinary Time
**Mercy for All**

| | | | |
|---|---|---|---|
| S 23 | Matthew 5:38-48 | StF276 | Ps 119:33-48 |
| M24 | Romans 11:13-24 | StF729 | Ps 119:113-128 |
| T 25 | Romans 11:25-36 | StF670 | Ps 119:129-144 |
| W26 | Romans 12:1-8 | StF382 | Ps 119:145-160 |
| T 27 | Romans 12:9-21 | StF603 | Ps 119:161-176 |
| F 28 | Romans 13:1-14 | StF637 | Ps 121 |
| S 1 | Romans 14:1-12 | StF737 | Ps 122 |

Week beginning 2 March
Week before Lent
**Peace and Joy in the Spirit**

| | | | |
|---|---|---|---|
| S 2 | Matthew 17:1-9 | StF259 | Ps 99 |
| M3 | Romans 14:13-23 | StF686 | Ps 126 |
| T 4 | Romans 15:1-13 | StF326 | Ps 132 |
| W5ab | Matthew 6:1-16, 16-21 | StF236 | Ps 51 |
| T 6 | Romans 15:14-33 | StF234 | Ps 125 |
| F 7ac | Romans 16:1-16 | StF240 | Ps 126 |
| S 8 | Romans 16:17-27 | StF637 | Ps 127 |

[ab=Ash Wednesday; ac=Women's World Day of Prayer]

Week beginning 9 March
1st in Lent
**Prayer in Temptation**

| | | | |
|---|---|---|---|
| S 9 | Matthew 4:1-11 | StF235 | Ps 91 |
| M10 | Leviticus 19:11-18 | StF237 | Ps 19 |
| T 11 | Isaiah 55:1-13 | StF663 | Ps 34:1-10 |
| W12 | Jonah 3:1-10 | StF696 | Ps 34:11-22 |
| T 13 | Matthew 7:1-12 | StF130 | Ps 138 |
| F 14 | Matthew 5:21-26 | StF691 | Ps 130 |
| S 15 | Matthew 5:43-48 | StF276 | Ps 1 |

Week beginning 16 March
2nd in Lent
**A Faithful God**

| | | | |
|---|---|---|---|
| S 16 | John 3:1-17 | StF503 | Ps 121 |
| M17 | Daniel 9:4-10 | StF238 | Ps 32 |
| T 18 | Isaiah 1:16-20 | StF79 | Ps 42 |
| W19ad | Matthew 1:18-25 | StF219 | Ps 89:26-36 |
| T 20 | Jeremiah 17:5-10 | StF455 | Ps 43 |
| F 21 | Jeremiah 18:18-20 | StF338 | Ps 130 |
| S 22 | Luke 15:11-32 | StF44 | Ps 143 |

[ad=Joseph of Nazareth]

Week beginning 23 March
3rd in Lent
**Enduring Love**

| | | | |
|---|---|---|---|
| S 23 | John 4:5-42 | StF556 | Ps 95 |
| M24 | 2 Kings 5:1-15 | StF453 | Ps 50:1-15 |
| T 25ae | Luke 1:26-38 | StF187 | Ps 40 |
| W26 | Deuteronomy 4:1-9 | StF665 | Ps 31 |
| T 27 | Jeremiah 7:23-28 | StF715 | Ps 103 |
| F 28 | Hosea 5:15–6:6 | StF680 | Ps 105:1-15 |
| S 29 | Hosea 14:1-9 | StF546 | Ps 101 |

[ae=Annunciation of the Lord]

Week beginning 30 March
4th in Lent
**Hearing the Word**

| | | | |
|---|---|---|---|
| S 30af | Luke 2:33-35 | StF119 | Ps 34 |
| M31 | Isaiah 65:17-21 | StF475 | Ps 23 |
| T 1 | Ezekiel 47:1-9 | StF377 | Ps 121 |
| W 2 | John 4:43-54 | StF650 | Ps 25 |
| T 3 | John 5:1-16 | StF466 | Ps 147 |
| F 4 | John 5:17-30 | StF364 | Ps 90 |
| S 5 | John 5:31-47 | StF55 | Ps 46 |

[af=Mothering Sunday]

## Week beginning 6 April
### Passion Week
**The Father Revealed**

| | | | |
|---|---|---|---|
| S 6 | John 11:1-45 | StF303 | Ps 130 |
| M7 | Numbers 21:4-9 | StF277 | Ps 24 |
| T 8 | Daniel 3:1-25 | StF278 | Ps 102:1-11 |
| W9 | Genesis 17:1-9 | StF280 | Ps 102:12-28 |
| T 10 | John 8:12-20 | StF281 | Ps 18:1-16 |
| F 11 | John 8:21-30 | StF282 | Ps 17 |
| S 12 | John 8:31-42 | StF287 | Ps 27 |

## Week beginning 13 April
### Holy Week
**Life Poured Out**

| | | | |
|---|---|---|---|
| S 13 | Matthew 27:11-54 | StF262 | Ps 19 |
| M14 | John 12:1-11 | StF566 | Ps 36 |
| T 15 | John 12:20-36 | StF361 | Ps 71 |
| W16 | John 13:21-32 | StF754 | Ps 70 |
| T 17ag | John 13:1-17, 31b-35 | St268 | Ps 116 |
| F 18ah | John 18:1–19:42 | StF273 | Ps 22 |
| S 19ai | John 19:38-42 | StF306 | Ps 4 |

[ag=Maundy Thursday; ah=Good Friday;
ai=Holy Saturday]

## Week beginning 20 April
### Easter Week
**The Day of Light**

| | | | |
|---|---|---|---|
| S 20aj | Matthew 28:1-10 | StF309 | Ps 118 |
| M21 | Daniel 6:1-28 | StF311 | Ps 16 |
| T 22 | Daniel 7:1-28 | StF313 | Ps 33 |
| W23 | Daniel 9:1-6 | StF314 | Ps 8 |
| T 24 | Daniel 9:20-27 | StF348 | Ps 145 |
| F 25 | Daniel 10:1-11:1 | StF418 | Ps 146 |
| S 26 | Daniel 12:1-13 | StF298 | Ps 153 |

[aj=Easter Day]

## Week beginning 27 April
### 2nd of Easter
**Resurrection and Life**

| | | | |
|---|---|---|---|
| S 27 | John 20:19-31 | StF314 | Ps 150 |
| M28 | Mark 13:5-13 | StF154 | Ps 148 |
| T 29ak | 1 Peter 1:1-12 | StF345 | Ps 73:1-14 |
| W30 | 1 Peter 1:13-25 | StF361 | Ps 73:15-28 |
| T 1al | John 14:1-14 | StF248 | Ps 139 |
| F 2 | 1 Peter 2:1-10 | StF456 | Ps 74:1-12 |
| S 3 | 1 Peter 2:11-25 | StF278 | Ps 74:13-23 |

[ak=Mark, Evangelist, trans.; al=Philip and James,
Apostles]

## Week beginning 4 May
### 3rd of Easter
**The Life of Faith**

| | | | |
|---|---|---|---|
| S 4 | Luke 24:13-35 | StF307 | Ps 116 |
| M5 | 1 Peter 3:1-12 | StF606 | Ps 1 |
| T 6 | 1 Peter 3:13-22 | StF214 | Ps 2:1-8 |
| W7 | 1 Peter 4:1-19 | StF520 | Ps 3 |
| T 8 | 1 Peter 5:1-14 | StF493 | Ps 4 |
| F 9 | 2 Peter 1:1-15 | StF147 | Ps 5:1-8 |
| S 10 | 2 Peter 1:16-18 | StF155 | Ps 6:1-9 |

## Week beginning 11 May
### 4th of Easter
**The Good Shepherd**

| | | | |
|---|---|---|---|
| S 11 | John 10:1-10 | StF480 | Ps 23 |
| M12 | 2 Peter 1:19-21 | StF155 | Ps 7:1-11 |
| T 13 | 2 Peter 3:1-7 | StF732 | Ps 9:1-10 |
| W14am | Acts 1:15-26 | StF664 | Ps 15 |
| T 15 | 2 Peter 3:8-10 | StF204 | Ps 10:1-12 |
| F 16 | 2 Peter 3:11-13 | StF205 | Ps 11:1-5 |
| S 17 | 2 Peter 3:14-18 | StF503 | Ps 12 |

[Christian Aid Week; am=Matthias, Apostle]

## Week beginning 18 May
### 5th of Easter
**Prayers of Faith**

| | | | |
|---|---|---|---|
| S 18 | John 14:1-14 | StF252 | Ps 148 |
| M19 | Luke 11:1-13 | StF528 | Ps 13 |
| T 20 | Joel 2:21-27 | StF370 | Ps 15 |
| W21 | Acts 14:8-18 | StF727 | Ps 16 |
| T 22 | Matthew 6:19-34 | StF130 | Ps 17 |
| F 23 | Jeremiah 14:1-9 | StF562 | Ps 18:1-16 |
| S 24an | Romans 5:1-11 | StF454 | Ps 130 |

[an=Conversions of John & Charles Wesley]

## Week beginning 25 May
### 6th of Easter
**Lord of All**

| | | | |
|---|---|---|---|
| S 25 | John 14:15-21 | StF372 | Ps 66 |
| M26 | Amos 1:1-15 | StF700 | Ps 19 |
| T 27 | Amos 2:1-16 | StF720 | Ps 20 |
| W28 | Amos 3:1-15 | StF718 | Ps 21:1-7 |
| T 29ao | Acts 1:6-11 | StF300 | Ps 24 |
| F 30 | Amos 4:1-13 | StF716 | Ps 23 |
| S 31 | Amos 5:1-17 | StF715 | Ps 25 |

[ao=Ascension Day]

| Week beginning 1 June | | | |
| 7th of Easter | | | |
| **Truth and Justice** | | | |
| S 1 | John 17:1-11 | StF315 | Ps 68 |
| M2 | Amos 5:18-24 | StF228 | Ps 26 |
| T 3 | Amos 6:1-14 | StF186 | Ps 27 |
| W4 | Amos 7:1-17 | StF157 | Ps 30 |
| T 5 | Amos 8:1-14 | StF703 | Ps 31:1-8 |
| F 6 | Amos 9:1-12 | StF732 | Ps 31:9-24 |
| S 7 | Amos 9:13-15 | StF741 | Ps 32 |

| Week beginning 8 June | | | |
| Pentecost | | | |
| **The Living Spirit** | | | |
| S 8ap | John 20:19-23 | StF371 | Ps 104 |
| M9 | Ezekiel 11:14-20 | StF370 | Ps 122 |
| T 10 | 1 Samuel 10:1-10 | StF372 | Ps 36:5-10 |
| W11aq | Acts 11:19-30 | StF678 | Ps 19 |
| T 12 | Micah 3:1-8 | StF375 | Ps 51:1-12 |
| F 13 | Exodus 35:30–31:1 | StF378 | Ps 33:1-6 |
| S 14 | Jeremiah 31:31-34 | StF380 | Ps 117 |

[ap=Day of Pentecost & Methodist Homes Sunday; aq=Barnabas, Apostle]

| Week beginning 15 June | | | |
| Trinity | | | |
| **Holy, Holy, Holy** | | | |
| S 15ar | Matthew 28:16-20 | StF5 | Ps 8 |
| M16 | Isaiah 6:1-8 | StF6 | Ps 93 |
| T 17 | Ephesians 1:3-14 | StF7 | Ps 97 |
| W18 | John 14:8-17 | StF11 | Ps 29 |
| T 19 | Galatians 4:1-7 | StF13 | Ps 145 |
| F 20 | Revelation 4:1-11 | StF9 | Ps 150 |
| S 21 | Revelation 15:1-4 | StF8 | Ps 100 |

[Refugee Week; ar=Trinity Sunday]

| Week beginning 22 June | | | |
| 12th in Ordinary Time | | | |
| **The Glory of the Lamb** | | | |
| S 22 | Matthew 10:24-39 | StF535 | Ps 86 |
| M23 | John 1:1-18 | StF212 | Ps 33:8-22 |
| T 24as | Luke 1:57-66, 80 | StF73 | Ps 80:1-7 |
| W25 | John 1:19-34 | StF182 | Ps 34:1-10 |
| T 26 | John 1:35-51 | StF350 | Ps 34:11-22 |
| F 27 | John 2:1-12 | StF192 | Ps 35:9-18 |
| S 28 | John 2:13-25 | StF247 | Ps 36 |

[as=Birth of John the Baptist]

| Week beginning 29 June | | | |
| 13th in Ordinary Time | | | |
| **Living Water** | | | |
| S29 | Matthew 10:40-42 | StF701 | Ps 13 |
| M30at | Matthew 16:13-19 | StF322 | Ps 125 |
| T 1 | John 3:1-15 | StF16 | Ps 85 |
| W2 | John 3:16-21 | StF59 | Ps 99 |
| T 3au | John 20:24-29 | StF316 | Ps 31:1-6 |
| F 4 | John 3:22-36 | StF432 | Ps 38:1-9 |
| S 5 | John 4:1-26 | StF300 | Ps 38:10-22 |

[at=Peter, Apostle, trans; au=Thomas, Apostle]

| Week beginning 6 July | | | |
| 14th in Ordinary Time | | | |
| **Sent by the Father** | | | |
| S 6 | Matthew 11:16-19, 25-30 | | |
| | | StF322 | Ps 45 |
| M7 | John 4:27-42 | StF566 | Ps 39 |
| T 8 | John 4:43-54 | StF195 | Ps 40:1-10 |
| W9 | John 5:1-18 | StF466 | Ps 41 |
| T 10 | John 5:19-29 | StF364 | Ps 42 |
| F 11 | John 5:30-47 | StF55 | Ps 43 |
| S 12 | John 6:1-15 | StF324 | Ps 44:1-8 |

| Week beginning 13 July | | | |
| 15th in Ordinary Time | | | |
| **Bread of the World** | | | |
| S 13av | Matthew 13:1-9, 18-23 | StF671 | Ps 65 |
| M14 | John 6:16-29 | StF125 | Ps 126 |
| T 15 | John 6:30-40 | StF713 | Ps 127 |
| W16 | John 6:41-51 | StF712 | Ps 132 |
| T 17 | John 6:52-59 | StF150 | Ps 135 |
| F 18 | John 6:60-71 | StF109 | Ps 136 |
| S 19 | John 7:1-13 | StF478 | Ps 138 |

[av=Action for Children Sunday]

| Week beginning 20 July | | | |
| 16th in Ordinary Time | | | |
| **The New Prophet** | | | |
| S 20 | Matthew 13:24-30, 56-43 | StF114 | Ps 139 |
| M21 | John 7:14-24 | StF675 | Ps 52 |
| T 22aw | Luke 8:1-3 | StF471 | Ps 63:1-8 |
| W23 | John 7:25-36 | StF12 | Ps 53 |
| T 24 | John 7:37-52 | StF248 | Ps 54 |
| F 25ax | Matthew 20:20-28 | StF486 | Ps 126 |
| S 26 | John 7:53–8:11 | StF613 | Ps 23 |

[aw=Mary Magdalene; ax=James, Apostle]

Week beginning 27 July
17th in Ordinary Time
**Honouring the Father**
S 27 Matthew 13:31-33, 44-52

|  |  |  |
|---|---|---|
|  | StF412 | Ps 105 |
| M28 John 8:12-20 | StF59 | Ps 55:1-8 |
| T 29 John 8:21-30 | StF361 | Ps 55:16-22 |
| W30 John 8:31-47 | StF485 | Ps 56 |
| T 31 John 8:48-59 | StF91 | Ps 57 |
| F 1 John 9:1-12 | StF582 | Ps 61 |
| S 2 John 9:13-23 | StF440 | Ps 62 |

Week beginning 3 August
18th in Ordinary Time
**The Shepherd's Glory**

| S 3 Matthew 14:13-21 | StF324 | Ps 17 |
|---|---|---|
| M4 John 9:24-41 | StF493 | Ps 64 |
| T 5 John 10:1-10 | StF480 | Ps 66 |
| W6ay 1 John 3:1-3 | StF261 | Ps 27 |
| T 7 John 10:11-21 | StF537 | Ps 67 |
| F 8 John 10:22-42 | StF535 | Ps 68:1-20 |
| S 9 John 11:1-16 | StF252 | Ps 68:24-35 |

[ay=The Transfiguration of the Lord]

Week beginning 10 August
19th in Ordinary Time
**Newness of Life**

| S 10 Matthew 14:22-33 | StF457 | Ps 85 |
|---|---|---|
| M11 John 11:17-27 | StF370 | Ps 119:1-16 |
| T 12 John 11:28-37 | StF420 | Ps 119:17-32 |
| W13 John 11:38-44 | StF647 | Ps 119:33-48 |
| T 14 John 11:45-57 | StF492 | Ps 119:49-64 |
| T 15az Galatians 4:4-7 | StF120 | Ps 45 |
| S 16 John 12:1-11 | StF56 | Ps 119:65-80 |

[az=The Blessed Virgin Mary]

Week beginning 17 August
20th in Ordinary Time
**Servant of All**

| S 17 Matthew 15:21-28 | StF251 | Ps 95 |
|---|---|---|
| M18 John 12:12-19 | StF263 | Ps 119:81-96 |
| T 19 John 12:20-50 | StF306 | Ps 119:97-112 |
| W20 John 13:1-11 | StF249 | Ps 119:113-128 |
| T 21 John 13:12-20 | StF244 | Ps 119:129-144 |
| F 22 John 13:21-30 | StF620 | Ps 119:145-160 |
| S 23 John 13:31-38 | StF398 | Ps 119:161-176 |

Week beginning 24 August
21st in Ordinary Time
**The Way to the Father**

| S 24 Matthew 16:13-20 | StF601 | Ps 124 |
|---|---|---|
| S 25ba Luke 22:24-30 | StF623 | Ps 145 |
| T 26 John 14:1-14 | StF470 | Ps 69:1-21 |
| W27 John 14:15-31 | StF372 | Ps 69:29-36 |
| T 28 John 15:1-17 | StF242 | Ps 72 |
| T 29bb Matthew 14:1-12 | StF732 | Ps 11 |
| S 30 John 15:18-27 | StF691 | Ps 75:1-7 |

[ba=Bartholomew, Apostle, trans;
bb=Beheading of John the Baptist]

We give thanks for lay leaders who exercise their faith in a local church;
for circuit officers as they lead God's people;
for the volunteer and paid staff who enable the East Anglia District to reach its goals.
We pray for new ventures in mission at Chesterton, Ramsey and St Neots;
for churches and circuits which are adopting new ways of working;
for the community at Wesley House, Cambridge during this time of transition and uncertainty.

**East Anglia District**

Chair
Graham Thompson

*Camp meeting, Wesley House, Cambridge (Geoffrey Farrar)*

For those who are abused
and those who abuse;
for those who are care-less about others
and those who are care-full;
for those who offer guidance through the dark
and those who endeavour to safeguard the vulnerable:
good Lord, we pray.

Loving God,
give hope
and a sense of your love and rightness
to the hurt.

May we all be led into safe and sound living.
Give us your strength for today;
your hope for tomorrow
and the light of your love to guide us in all things. Amen.

*Elizabeth Hall, National Safeguarding Adviser,
Church of England and Methodist Church*

Light of the world, you have drowned our darkness by your presence.
You give purpose to each new day, and hope for today and tomorrow.
Saviour Christ, help us so to shine with your light and demonstrate your hope
such that your presence in us brings light and hope to others. Amen.

*Graham Thompson, East Anglia District Chair*

God whose mystery no tongue can describe and whose thoughts no speech can utter; receive the praise of your whole creation and illumine our souls with the glory of your presence, for you live and reign, now and for ever. Amen.

*Gregory of Nazianzus (c.329-389)*

**Middle East Council of Churches**

**Iran**

**Syria**

**Lebanon**

**Egypt**

**Israel/Palestine**

We give thanks to God for the renewed commitment to an ecumenical spirit through the **Middle East** Council of Churches. We pray for the World Council of Churches programme, Ecumenical Accompaniment Programme in **Palestine and Israel** (EAPPI).

We give thanks for the opening of the Methodist Liaison Office in Jerusalem, run jointly by the United Methodist Church and the Methodist Church in Britain, endorsed by the World Methodist Council and the Methodist Church in Nigeria. We pray that it will enable the Methodist family to link with and experience the life of Christians in the region and to work for peace, healing and reconciliation.

*Palestinian Easter procession (EAPPI/ Mickael Hjort)*

> Light of the world,
> let your light shine throughout your earth.
> Let it reach the dark corners where evildoers hide,
> so that all can see them for what they are.
>
> Hope of the world,
> bring hope to people who are suffering from poverty,
> homelessness and the aftermath of military action.
> In particular, we think of the people of the **Middle East**.
> Let your light shine on their leaders and
> touch their hearts with your love. Amen.
>
> *Barbara Sigley, church steward,*
> *Wolverhampton and Shrewsbury*

*EAPPI are looking for volunteer human rights monitors to help put prayers for a just peace in Israel-Palestine into action.*
*Email eappi@quaker.org.uk for more information.*

God of Abraham, have mercy on the people of Israel/Palestine.
Open a door of hope in the Holy Land,
that those who, in enmity and bitterness,
disown and dishonour your covenant
may turn their hearts to your righteousness and justice,
steadfast love and mercy,
and become a source of blessing to their neighbours
and to all nations. Amen.

*Inspired by Hosea 2:15–20*
*Colin Smith, supernumerary minister, Sankey Valley Circuit*

We give thanks for the green shoots of change and growth which are evident in the life of the Methodist Church in the Isle of Man;

for new ways of meeting old needs, in particular the work with Scripture Union and the unfolding of the Messy Church project in Ramsey and Sulby;

for growing confidence in the development of new structures which will enable the people of the district to work together to fulfil God's mission on the island.

We pray for those in leadership on the Isle of Man as they continue to discern the future shape of work there;

for the work of the Scripture Union Mission Trust which provides gap year workers in many of the district's churches and takes a lead in schools work;

for a spiritual re-awakening across all the denominations on the Isle of Man.

### Isle of Man District

**Rheynn Ellan Vannin Yn Agglish Haasilagh**

Chair
Richard Hall

*The Thousla Cross, Isle of Man, commemorates brave men who risked their lives to save the crew of a wrecked French ship (Richard Hall)*

> Lord, you have called us to be a people of hope who offer a rescuing hand to those in dark places. Give us the courage to make ourselves vulnerable in order that those we serve may come to know the light of your love. Amen.
>
> *Richard Hall, Isle of Man District Chair*

God of hope, we thank you that you made men and women with contrasting but complementary characteristics;

for the unique insights and abilities that you have given to women;

for Methodist Women in Britain, which offers so many opportunities to women to be part of something larger than themselves and the congregations to which they belong;

for the opportunities Methodist Women in Britain gives to women to study and to explore, to receive news and to take action, to pray and to stand in solidarity with women worldwide.

Help us to continue to offer hope to our sisters, who are struggling under the burdens of poverty and deprivation, exploitation and oppression, and to continue to take action in support of the United Nations Millennium Development Goals.

*Elizabeth Burroughs, Methodist representative, National Committee, Women's World Day of Prayer\**

*\*Women's World Day of Prayer 7 March 2014*

47

## Praying with Christians in the Indian Subcontinent

In our need, O Lord, we come to the Divine Physician, as thirsty to the fountain of life, as blind to your healing light, as beggars to stretch out our hands, as pilgrims to see you face to face. Amen.

*Thomas Aquinas (c.1225-1274)*

**Church of Pakistan**

Moderator
Sammy Azariah

Mission Partners
ed  Rachel Ullmer

**Church of Bangladesh**

Moderator
Paul Sarkar

Mission Partners
n  Pat Jamison
[+ CofS, CMS, CWM]

We pray for all Christians in **Pakistan,** especially those unjustly accused under the blasphemy laws, and those in prison or in hiding;
for communities such as the Joseph Colony in Lahore, which have been attacked;
for their persecutors;
for those newly elected to power in Pakistan, that they may do whatever they can to enable their people to live peacefully alongside each other, no matter what their faith.

*Steve Pearce, WCR Partnership Coordinator, Asia-Pacific*

We give thanks for the work of the Christian Study Centre in **Pakistan** which has been successfully promoting inter faith relations and carrying out various peace-building activities. We pray for Christine Amjad-Ali, the centre's director, and for the people who use the centre, that they will become more positive, self-confident and generous in their faith.

We give thanks for **Bangladesh**, with all the diversity it brings; for the work carried out by the Church of Bangladesh in both rural and urban areas;
for the good standard of education provided by Church of Bangladesh schools.
We pray for hope in a land where many feel hopeless, and a clear voice where many feel that what they say goes unheard and strength for those who feel weak;
for insight for national and local government leaders, that all the decisions they make will be fair and just;
for all the regions where the Church works tirelessly to help local people, through hostels for boys and girls, health advice and disease prevention through the Community Health Department, development work with women's groups, climate change and disaster preparedness, human-trafficking prevention and projects with street children.

*Pat Jamison, mission partner, Bangladesh*

*Hope for the future as a street child learns to read in Dhaka, Bangladesh (Karen Drayton)*

Lord God, we pray for the beautiful city of Belfast:
for peace where there is unrest;
for love where there is division or suspicion;
for economic strength for her and for her people.

We pray for wisdom for peacemakers
and for the anointing of your Spirit,
that their words may have influence.

We pray that Christians will be a blessing
in their communities and across the city.

We look for the day
when all will owe their primary allegiance to you, loving God,
and for the day
when Belfast will be known as a place of peace. Amen.

*Heather Morris, former Belfast District Superintendent*

**Belfast District (Ireland)**

Superintendent
Harold Agnew

---

We give thanks for the encouragement of working collaboratively in the Leeds District in ways that release the gifts of many;
for the reshaping of circuits that has strengthened teams of lay and ordained people for mission and ministry;
for all who work for the National Health Service, and for the well-being of the most vulnerable in our midst.
We pray for wisdom in reshaping the Methodist presence in Leeds city centre, alongside ecumenical partners;
for the developing ecumenical chaplaincy at Leeds Bradford Airport, and for all whose work contributes to safer travel by air, road and rail;
for the cities, towns and villages of Yorkshire that will host the initial stages of the Tour de France in July 2014.

**Leeds District**

Chair
Liz Smith

God of the past, who knows our unique histories,
God of the future, stirring us to plan and to dream,
we respond to your invitation in this present moment
to kindle the flame of your hope within us and around us:
for it is your hope-filled presence, and your eternal light
that scatter the darkness from the paths before us
to guide our feet in the paths of peace. Amen.

*Liz Smith, Leeds District Chair*

## Praying with Christians in India

Let us fear you, O Lord, beyond whom there is none more holy; love you beyond whom there is none more loveable; glorify you beyond whom there is none more worthy of praise and long for you beyond whom there is none more desirable; and grant that thus fearing, loving, glorifying and longing we may see you, face to face; through Christ our Lord. Amen.

*Desiderius Erasmus (1466-1536)*

**Church of North India (CNI)**

Moderator
Philip Marandih

**Church of South India (CSI)**

Moderator
G Devakadasham

We give thanks for all the blessings and divine guidance showered upon the **Church of North India** (CNI); for all the partners who support the CNI Synod, enabling it to reach out to the most vulnerable communities across India. We pray for the leadership of the CNI: the Moderator, the Most Revd Dr Philip Phembuar Marandih; the Deputy Moderator, the Rt Revd Pradeep Kumar Samantaroy; the General Secretary, Alwan Masih and the Acting Treasurer Prem Masih; for the Church's work with children, and particularly the PDS Hostels. *

*Alwan Masih, General Secretary, Church of North India Synod*

We pray for unique, often-misunderstood, India;
for girls to be appreciated and have a sense of their own value;
for women to be free of violence;
for men to find satisfying and sustaining work;
for young people to follow their vision to create a better world;
for strength of character for those with wealth and power;
for a way out of bribery and corruption;
for honest land transactions especially to prevent the
    exploitation of tribal peoples;
for Christians to be worthy of the trust placed in them.

*Shubhro, Elisabeth, Nick, Sandra, and Karen,*
*Khristiya Seva Niketan Hospital, Sarenga, West Bengal, India*

*Sudamanagar Kindergarten, Nagpur, Central India (Linda Crossley)*

As the lamp is lit,
let us pray that the flame of God's loving presence
may spring up in our hearts
and transform us by the knowledge of his glory
in the face of Jesus Christ. Amen.

*In the tradition of the Church of South India*

*Sandra Clack, India Link Committee,*
*Churches Together in All Lincolnshire*

*PDS = Parent, Diocese, Synod, where one third of the cost is met by each party to enable poorer children to attend good schools.

As the Lincolnshire District reflects on its policy Towards a 2020 Vision, we give thanks that Methodist identity across the county is being strengthened, cooperation with partners is becoming more meaningful and engagement with the wider community more effective.

We pray for those who are taking part in the Step Forward programme;

for those who help in the growing number of food banks;

for those involved in schools and other places of education;

for those who exercise chaplaincy across society and a variety of workplaces.

**Lincolnshire District**

Chair
Bruce Thompson

*(Bruce Thompson)*

> O Lord, we are often miserable, as though without hope.
> Lift us into your light and help us to smile
> so that others may see you in us. Amen.
> *Donald Bullen, supernumerary minister, Liverpool*

Let us find Hope in one another, for Hope is the Divine Within.
To be Hope-full is to know true fullness, but to be without Hope is to be lost and afraid,
for Hope is eternal peace and light.
Hope is expressed in those who live with integrity
    and to seek integrity enables Hope to rise from within.
Hope believes in us and believes in our being able to overcome all adversity
through a sense of Hope-fulness.
As Hope believes in us then we should believe that others too
    can achieve great things.
To have Hope in one another binds us together in a wholly new and dynamic way.
Hope is the Divine Within and those who nurture Hope in themselves and in others
develop a bond with the Divine.
Hope is present because,
    come the day of trauma, the day of grief, the day when all else seems lost,
    Hope remains and will sustain us, pointing beyond the present.
To have Hope is to glimpse eternal joy
but to be without Hope is to find that fear is very real.
When others see Hope in us we can draw on their affirmation
    and in turn find and nurture Hope in others.
If we want Hope for ourselves yet deny others a sense of Hope-fullness
    then we cannot possibly be fulfilled and all will be a sham.

*Inspired by 1 John 4*
*Bruce Thompson, Lincolnshire District Chair*
*taken from A Testament of Hope, transforming life in troubled times,*
*Church in the Market Place Publications, 2011*

## Praying with Christians in Asia

Grant to me, O Lord, the penitence of the Publican who dared not raise his eyes to heaven, the longing of the Prodigal who wanted to return home and the wisdom of the Merchant who surrendered all to possess the kingdom. Amen.

*Rabbula of Edessa (d.435)*

**Myanmar**
The Methodist Church
of Upper Myanmar
Methodist President
Zaw Win Aung

**Scholarship Student**
Fung Mang
(in Singapore)

**Nepal**
The United Mission to
Nepal (UMN)

**Director of the UMN**
Mark Galpin

**Mission Partners**
sd/p Paul and Sarah
Wright, Jack and
Asha
p Malcolm° [+CofS]
and Cati Ramsay

**Scholarship Student**
Nalome Rongong
(in Britain)

*Sang Bik Cem, former SALT student from Myanmar hard at work in Japan (Steven Cutting, ARI )*

Let us pray for the Kachin people of **Myanmar** who are suffering from poverty as fighting continues between government forces and the KIA (Kachin Independent Army); for those who have lost their lives; for the many people who have lost their homes; for the Muslim Rohingya minority who live in the Rakhine area of Myanmar who are being persecuted by the Buddhist majority.

*Fung Mang,*
*SALT student from Myanmar*

For the ongoing movement, Christian Commitment for Building a New **Nepal**. May the Church continue to be bold enough to assign resources to address major social problems, including corruption, lack of education, caste discrimination, unemployment and violence against women, and fulfil their commitment towards the building of a new Nepal by bridging the gap between the Church, civil society and the Government of Nepal.

> Hear us, O Lord.
> Open our hurt to your healing power,
> Pour in the balm of your presence and
> Encourage us to move on. Amen.
>
> *Jenny Park, supernumerary minister,*
> *Rotherham and Dearne Valley Circuit*

We give thanks for the life, energy and hope of the City Centre Network serving Warrington, Liverpool, Birkenhead and Ellesmere Port;
for the Covenant relationship now entered into by the seven districts of the North West, which commits them to working ever more closely across district boundaries;
for the work and witness of chaplains and chaplaincies in the workplace, universities, prisons and hospitals.
We pray for work with the schools of the district, in particular with the Methodist schools;
for the ministry of hope offered to survivors of abuse through the work of CASAI (Church Action on Sexual Abuse Issues);
for the development of a mission to bring hope to those suffering hardship and deprivation in inner-city areas.

**Liverpool District**

**Chair**
James Booth

The Sheppard-Worlock memorial: hope for a shared future in Liverpool (Liz Smith)

> Loving, living Lord,
> in Jesus you come into this world in love,
> light shining in our darkness.
>
> So we dare to hope,
> for in your love and light, hope, too, is born,
> hope which is real,
> for this world and all its people, for me.
>
> So help me to live this day in hope,
> your gift in Jesus, in whose name I pray. Amen.
> *James Booth, Liverpool District Chair*

Gracious and generous God, you have told us through your prophets Isaiah and Micah of a time when nations shall no longer learn war, and shall not lift up arms against each other. And yet, Lord, we find little trace of this being fulfilled in our world today, where nations spend billions of dollars on weapons while children starve and thousands die every year in violent conflict. Awaken your Church, Holy One, to listen to the voice of prophecy. Stir up our congregations to participate in this struggle for peace, until your promises come true, and all people dwell in peace and safety, through Jesus Christ, Prince of Peace. Amen.
*John Hull, Honorary Professor of Practical Theology, The Queen's Foundation and Emeritus Professor of Religious Education, University of Birmingham*

## Praying with Christians in Asia

Forgive my sins, O Lord, both past and present. Forgive the sins of my soul and the sins of my body. Forgive the sins I have done to please myself, and those I have done to please others. Forgive my casual sins, and my deliberate sins. Forgive the sins I have sought to hide from myself and those I have presumed to hide, even from you; and all of these for your love and your mercies' sake. Amen.

*Thomas Wilson (1663-1755)*

### Indonesia
Methodist Bishop
Darwis Manurung

### Sri Lanka
Methodist President
Albert Jebanesan

### Mission Partners
p Mervyn° and
    Claudette Kilpatrick
th/ed Mannie° and
    Lynne Jacob

We give thanks for the work of the Methodist Seminary in Medan, North Sumatra, **Indonesia**, in training lay workers and candidates for ordained ministry.
We pray for the students there, that the light of Christ will lead them into a deeper understanding of scriptural holiness, and empower them with the ability to exercise a fruitful ministry in their future appointments.
We pray for the Chinese-speaking Methodist Church in Indonesia;
for a strengthening of unity with colleagues in the Indonesian-speaking Methodist Church;
that more Chinese-speaking ministers will be raised up;
that the Indonesian Methodist Church will profit from its links with the world Methodist family, and contribute to the well-being of that family.

*Geoffrey Senior, former mission partner, Indonesia*

*The Revd Dr Jerome Sahabandhu, Principal of Theological College of Lanka, with his family, Inoka, Nisal and Shalomi (Lynn Jacob)*

We thank you, O Lord, for the blessings of many natural resources and the beauty of the 'Pearl of the Indian Ocean', **Sri Lanka**. We give thanks for the work of the Methodist Church and all other Christian Churches who bring Christ's incarnate love to others. We pray for an enduring peace with justice which will enhance people's lives and we pray for everyone to feel secure and to live with dignity. Lord, grant your divine love so that there might be forgiveness and renewal in the lives of all Sri Lanka's communities.

*Leslie Daareju, minister, Methodist Church of Sri Lanka and former student, The Queen's Foundation, Birmingham*

We give thanks for new initiatives in mission in the Manchester and Stockport District, especially in youth and children's work;
for the emerging district networks which support work in larger churches, in the creative arts, with younger adults and with those engaged in Fresh Expressions;
for the new district agency, Transforming Churches and Communities, as it helps churches to engage more effectively with their local communities;
for Methodist International House which provides a safe and welcoming space for students from all over the world.
We pray for the work of the District Leadership Team;
for the developing partnership of the seven districts in the North West;
for the new MHA homes being opened in the district;
for the new Rural Development Enabler in the three Peak Park districts;
for all those involved in theological education during this time of radical change.

**Manchester and Stockport District**

Chair
Keith Davies

Creator God, who in the work of creation commanded light to shine out of darkness, deliver us from the darkness of sin, ignorance and unbelief and fill us with hope in you and your loving, creative purposes.

Saving God, whose light was revealed in the humility and obedience of your Son, our saviour Jesus Christ, may we, inspired by the wonder of your saving love, commit our lives to your service and the service of others.

Life-giving God, in a world where many are without hope, help us so to live in your light and proclaim the good news of your love, that we may bring light and hope to all who live in darkness. Amen.

*Keith Davies, Manchester and Stockport District Chair*

Lord of all worlds,
your love knows no boundaries;
not of ocean, mountain or wilderness,
but reaches out constantly, hopefully, willingly.

Help us we pray,
to see your love in unexpected places
and to respond with our whole selves. Amen.

*Fiona Green, local preacher, Ashbourne Circuit*

55

## Praying with Christians in Asia

Come to us, O Christ, as the wind that blows the autumn leaves, as the song that soothes the troubled child, as the melody that lifts the anxious spirit, and fill us with affection for you that is unbounded, desire for you that is unrestrained and a yearning for you that throws caution to the winds, and this for your own love's sake. Amen.

*Richard Rolle (c.1290-1349)*

**Singapore**

Methodist Bishop
Wee Boon Hup

**Malaysia**

Methodist Bishop
Ong Hwai Teik

Scholarship Students
Dennis Raj
Maylia Staychi Likun
(both in Britain)

We give thanks to God for the vibrancy of the Methodist Church in **Singapore**, its deep-rooted sense of heritage and world connexionalism, its passion for discipleship, mission and social holiness which are particularly evident in the development of churches, youth work, education and women's ministry.

We pray for the Bishop of the General Conference, the Revd Dr Wee Boon Hup, in his initial stage of office and for the presidents of the Chinese, Tamil and Trinity Conferences that they may have wisdom and vision to lead;

for renewed response and training for ordained ministry;

for family relationships tested when those from other traditions become Christians.

*Lily Twist, Methodist Synod in Scotland Chair*

We give thanks for the smooth election of the new officers of the General Conference of the Methodist Church in **Malaysia**;

for the leadership, hard work and dedication of Bishop Hwa Yung who has served the Methodist Church in Malaysia as bishop for eight years;

for freedom of religion for all citizens in a predominantly Muslim country.

We pray for the new leaders in the Methodist Church in Malaysia: Bishop Thangavelu Jeyakumar of the Trinity Annual Conference and President Hii Kong Hock of the Sabah Provisional Annual Conference;

for the political leaders of Malaysia, that with integrity and hard work they will serve the country according to God's ways;

for a solution to the issues around the use of the Malay language, which are affecting the printing of the Bible in Malay.

*Michael William, acting editor,*
*Pelita Methodist Church magazine, Malaysia*

*Bringing light and hope to Singapore: Lily Twist with John Wesley (Peter Teo)*

We give thanks for ECG North East (Equipping, Calling, Going: a day of celebration, teaching and workshops) and the inspiration and encouragement it brings to so many; for district, circuit and local church administrators and for all the work they do behind the scenes; for the return of the Lindisfarne Gospels to the North East and the opportunities this has provided for the living Word.
We pray for Together, a mission initiative by the district to the district and for the district in autumn 2013; for ecumenical partners in the North East who have recently taken up new appointments, particularly for Justin Welby, the new Archbishop of Canterbury; for The Ark@Crawcrook, a church, play centre, sensory room and café which seeks to connect with, and support, the local and wider community and to offer fresh ways of engaging local people with faith and the gospel.

**Newcastle upon Tyne District**

**Chair**
Leo Osborn

*The Ark*
*(© Shaun Hutchinson,*
*© Mike Broadfield,*
*used with permission)*

Lord Jesus Christ, light of the nations and
hope of all who put their trust in you:
in darkness shine!
In despair lift up!
Where the way seems impossible, show us your ways!
And with all your people keep us
    joyful in hope,
    patient in affliction
    and faithful in prayer
until your kingdom comes. Amen.

*Leo Osborn, Newcastle District Chair*

We pray for members of our Church; young, old and in between.
We pray that each one would feel valued and at home.
We pray that every person would feel a sense of purpose and be able to contribute.
Thank you God that you work through us; we give our lives to you.
We pray for people who work with children, young people and families on our behalf.
We ask that you would guide them in their work and remind us to cheer them on.
Thank you God that you welcome us all into your family.
Help us to be welcoming, supportive, and to see people the way you see them. Amen.

*Hayley Moss, Methodist Youth President, 2012/2013*

## Praying with Christians in East Asia

Be to us, O Lord, the closest of our companions, our everlasting love and our enduring happiness. Through your Spirit, create in us holy fire and purity of life, that loving you above all things and our neighbours ardently, we may come to the glories of your everlasting kingdom; through Christ our Lord. Amen.

*Thomas à Kempis (1380-1471)*

### China

President of China Christian Council
Gao Feng

Amity Teachers
Mina Kelly
*Amity is a Chinese non-government organisation founded by Christians.*

### Hong Kong
(Special Administrative Region of China)

Methodist President
Tin-yau Yuen

Mission Partner
p/ed  Howard and
    Rosie Mellor°

*Hope in the Word in China (Ian Groves)*

We thank you that, though nations may rise and fall, your goodness, mercy, and love for all creation endure forever.
We thank you for the economic rise of **China**, which is allowing millions to lift themselves out of crushing poverty and live lives of dignity and self-respect.
We thank you for the rise of the Church in China, which offers a message of hope and love to those struggling to come to terms with dizzying changes and ever-growing material and social pressures.
Lord Jesus Christ, we pray for unity and reconciliation among all who bear your name in China, especially between members of the registered and unregistered churches and between Catholics and Protestants.

*Ian Groves, former Amity teacher*

We thank God for the ministry of the Revd Dr Howard Mellor in **Hong Kong** and the ministry among Chinese that has flourished in different parts of Britain with the love and support of British Methodists;
for the steady growth of youth ministry in Hong Kong and the increasing commitment and enhanced capability of youth workers who are supported by regular training;
for contact with Christian Churches in Wenzhou, China, where the Church is flourishing and facing the demands of building ever bigger churches, nurturing new leaders and training clergy;
for the ministry of Lillian Leung, who went out to the Philippines in 2010 and is now undergoing linguistic training in Payap University in Thailand in order to serve in literacy education in South East Asia in the future.

*Tin-yau Yuen, Methodist President, Hong Kong*

We give thanks for the Spirit of God calling churches to new mission opportunities in the Down District; for God's people who seek to follow Jesus; for faithful leaders who serve beyond the call of duty. We pray for a renewed understanding of what it is to be missional, and for peace and reconciliation in Ireland.

> May you experience God's
>     vast, infinite, indestructible, expansive love,
>     that has been yours all along.
> May you discover this love is as wide as the sky,
> and as small as the cracks in your heart
>     that no-one else knows about,
> and may you know deep in your bones
>     that you are welcome, invited and loved. Amen.
>                 *Brian Anderson, Down District Superintendent*

**Down District (Ireland)**

Superintendent
Brian Anderson

*Love as wide as the sky*
*(Paul Martin)*

We give thanks for all the children in the churches and Methodist schools of the Lancashire District, for those who work among them and for the initiative of the Child-Friendly Church Award;
for signs of hope as younger people respond to God's call to leadership within church and community;
for developing partnerships following the recent District Mission Team visits to Papua New Guinea, Sierra Leone and Uruguay and the challenge and hope they offer.
We pray for those who offer the light of Christ in some of Lancashire's most needy communities, through care of the homeless in Blackpool, refugees in Blackburn, the poor in Morecambe, the abused in Preston, that they may continue to challenge the structures which cause these problems;
for the Lancashire District's Year of Evangelism, that it will make the members of the district bold in sharing the love of Christ;
for the former District Chair, the Revd Stephen Poxon, as he embarks on a new phase of life;
for the new District Chair, Paul Davis, that he will be enabled by the Holy Spirit to offer vision and leadership to God's people across Lancashire.

**Lancashire District**

Chair
Paul Davis

Great, O Lord, is your kingdom, your power and your glory; great are your works, your wonders and your praises; great also is your wisdom, your goodness, your justice and your mercy, and for all these we bless you and magnify your holy name, for ever and ever. Amen.

*George Wither (1588-1667)*

**Korean Methodist Church**

Interim President
Bishop Ki-Taek Kim

**Japan**

Moderator of the Kyodan, the United Church of Christ in Japan
Hideo Ishibashi

**Mission Partners**
ed Sheila Norris
ed Daniel and Yasuko Dellming, Momoko, Daisuke and Yoko

*Members of a Korean Methodist Church house fellowship group (Ward Jones)*

We give thanks for emerging young male and female leaders within the Korean Methodist Church (KMC);
for the work of the KMC Boards of Mission and Social Responsibility;
for the work of the KMC among Korean communities in Britain and across Europe.
We pray for **South Korea**'s first female president, Park Geun-hye, and her pledge to pursue "national reconciliation" and improve "economic democracy" and social welfare;
for President Kim Jong-un in **North Korea**, that he will be open to dialogue with the world beyond his own borders;
for fruitful cooperation among the major world powers and all who work for a reduction in the tensions between the governments of the North and South;
for renewed life and vitality across the churches at a time when dynamic growth has become an exception rather than the norm.

*Ward Jones, Bristol District Chair and Honorary Bishop, JoonAng Conference of the Korean Methodist Church*

We give thanks for all the support, prayers and encouragement which have been given to **Japan** from around the world to carry out reconstruction projects in the areas affected by the tsunami and earthquake of 2011.
We pray for the 300,000 people still residing in temporary housing;
for missionaries working in Japan and devoting themselves to youth evangelism.
We pray that the United Church of Christ in Japan and Christians in Japan as a whole may seek God's way to spread the gospel to the people of Japan and that the country of Japan may follow the way God wishes her to go and contribute to world peace.

*Marina Sugiyama, Ecumenical Ministries, The United Church of Christ in Japan*

We give thanks for those circuits engaged in reshaping for mission who are now seeing the early signs of growth; for circuit and church administrators who make such a difference to circuit life.

We pray for the 'church in the community', a fresh expression of church in the Nottingham East Circuit which meets in a local school and which is now seeking to become a church in its own right;

for those engaged in Discipling courses, Alpha and Mission-shaped intro and ministry;

for the MHA offices and homes in the district, for those who work in them and for the residents of the homes;

for the many links with Action for Children in the district, that these may make a difference for as long as it takes.

**Nottingham and Derby District**

**Chair**
Loraine Mellor

Lord God, as we wake,
we remember that this day is yours.
You bring to us the hope of each new day
and fresh opportunities to heal a broken world.
May we hear in many places your whisper,
inspiring us to pray and act
with the compassion of Jesus,
the light of the world,
in whose name we pray. Amen.

Lord God, as we go to sleep,
we remember that this night belongs to you.
We bring to you the joys of the day,
along with our tiredness,
our anxieties,
our concerns
and the regret of things left undone.
May we hear your whisper granting us peace
and a good night's rest;
through Christ, our risen light, we pray. Amen.

*Inspired by Psalm 74:16*
*Paul Hill, Nottingham and Derby District Deputy Chair*

*Yours is the day...*

*...yours also the night*
*(Geoffrey Farrar)*

61

## Praying with Christians in Australia and New Zealand

Let me prefer your presence, O God, to all other company. Let me exalt your name above all others names, and let me love your will beyond all other desires; for the sake of Jesus Christ. Amen.

*Thérèse of Lisieux (1873-1897)*

**The Uniting Church in Australia (UCA)**

President
Rex Nathan

**Aotearoa/ New Zealand**

Methodist President
Andrew Dutney

We give thanks for the worship, witness and service that is carried out by the congregations and agencies of the Uniting Church across **Australia**;
for Frontier Services, which celebrated 100 years of ministry to remote areas of Australia in 2012, as it continues to expand its work;
for UnitingWorld's partnerships with churches in the Pacific, Asia and Africa;
for the many people who have migrated to Australia and formed congregations within the Uniting Church there.
We pray for the Uniting Aboriginal and Islander Christian Congress within the Uniting Church as it seeks to deal with issues relating to indigenous people;
for the work of UnitingJustice, especially with asylum seekers and refugees;
for new mission and evangelism initiatives which share the gospel with people in secular, multicultural Australia.

*Chris Walker, National Consultant for Theology and Discipleship, Uniting Church in Australia*

Christ in a Maori cloak,
St Faith's Church,
Uhinemutu, Rotorua, NZ
(Elizabeth Hoyle)

God of Hope, we pray for **New Zealand**, country of contrasts, of towering mountains, dramatic volcanoes, peaceful lakes, of earthquakes and heartache.
Restoring God, be with the people of Christchurch, people of hope, people of courage continuing to rebuild shattered homes and shattered lives.
God of light and hope bless your country of New Zealand.

*Elizabeth Hoyle, Wharfedale and Aireborough Circuit*

---

**A prayer for new vision**
Christ who loves mercy, soften my humanity with your holiness. I come to you to find new dimensions for life. Enlarge my spirit, expand the limits I impose on you and give me new sacraments of sacrifice and caring. Let me trust my visions that I may see, through windows of prayer, that unending life where I am always yours. Amen.
*Selwyn Veater, prayer co-ordinator, Dorset Gardens Methodist Church, Brighton*

We give thanks for the strides made by circuits in the Northampton District in regrouping for mission through setting mission-focused priorities, making new appointments and moving away from redundant buildings and systems;
for fruitful engagement in local communities through providing food and a welcome to the poor, through projects which promote multifaith and multicultural harmony and through a wide variety of chaplaincies;
We pray for effective ways for churches to break out of the bonds of outdated customs and practices and to find new hope in God's new way for them;
for those in leadership, that they may be inspired by God's vision for today and find courage to lead in that way;
for all people in the Northampton District in both urban and rural settings, the affluent and the poor, the indigenous and those from elsewhere in the world, that they may find their deepest needs met in healthy communities and that all may see the light of Christ.

**Northampton District**

Chair
Peter Hancock

## Prayer for a fellowship group

O Lord God of us all,
in our gathering today,
may you be included in our thoughts, spoken and unspoken,
may we notice you through our discussions with each other,
may you be part of the conversation,
and may we leave this meeting knowing that
your words and ideas have been part of our sharing. Amen.

*Annette Sampson, local preacher, Birmingham*

---

The field looks hard and bare, but even now the seed grows beneath the ground.
The land is parched and barren, but even now a cloud makes its way over the horizon.
The tomb is sealed, but even now new life is breaking the bonds of death.
Lord of creation and resurrection, you
    bring life where there was none,
    turn the desert into a garden and overwhelm death,
    bring food to the hungry,
        water to the thirsty,
            peace to the troubled
and joy to the hearts of men, women and children throughout the earth.
May the heavens burst forth in praise of Father, Son and Holy Spirit. Amen.

*Peter Hancock, Northampton District Chair*

O God, who has prepared for those who love you, such good things as pass our understanding: pour into our hearts such love towards you, that we, loving you above all things, may obtain your promises, which exceed all that we can desire; through Jesus Christ our Lord. Amen.

*Book of Common Prayer (1662)*

### United Church of the Solomon Islands

**Moderator**
Wilfred Kurepitu

**Mission Partners**
d/d  Graham and Jenny Longbottom

**Scholarship Student**
Mike Visara (in Papua New Guinea)

### United Church in Papua New Guinea

**Moderator**
Bernard Siai

**Scholarship Students**
Gairo Alaimao
Walo Temu
Ralai Vali
 (all in Singapore)
Sam Mea (in Britain)

**Mission Partner**
ed  Wande Ebofin

*Donations of baby clothes at the Helena Goldie hospital, Solomon Islands (Graham Longbottom)*

We pray for leaders of the United Church of the **Solomon Islands**, especially the Moderator, the Revd Wilfred Kurepitu and the recently appointed General Secretary, Eddison Kotomae. We remember the many schools, the three hospitals and the Helena Goldie College of Nursing which are run by the United Church (formerly the Methodist Church there).
We pray for the 75 medical students from the Solomon Islands currently studying in Cuba, that they will be able to play their part in the expansion and development of the health service of the nation when they begin returning home in 2014.
We remember those affected by religious differences in the West Province, some of whom are the victims of violence and others of whom have had to leave their homes and villages, which has disrupted health care and education.

*Graham Longbottom, mission partner, Solomon Islands*

We praise and thank the Lord for the Assembly and Development Office of the United Church of **Papua New Guinea**, led by the Moderator, the Revd Bernard Siai.
We pray for insight in the implementation of the Development Plan for Education;
for blessing on the schools and colleges: Rarongo (which specialises in theology and mission), Gaulim (education), Malmaluan (skills and leadership) and Salamo (rural health science);
for the Revd Garo Kilagi, the new principal of the Theological College at Rarongo and his family as they settle back into life in Papua New Guinea after seven years of service in Lancashire.

*John North, Lancashire District World Mission Team*

We give thanks for new partnerships between the Plymouth and Exeter District and the Cuttak Diocese of the Church of North India;

for the beginnings of ecumenical work in the new town of Cranbrook, east of Exeter, where a Methodist minister has been appointed as an ecumenical minister, in Anglican-led ecumenical work.

We pray for rural circuits who are facing reductions in staffing because of financial constraints and difficulties in attracting ministers to the district;

for farming communities suffering because of TB infections in cattle which mean that herds are put under movement restrictions and cannot be sold but still have to be fed;

for the work of the district's rural pastoral worker as he meets farmers at the markets of north and north-west Devon.

**Plymouth and Exeter District**

Chair
Peter Pillinger

*(Paul Martin)*

Generous God, your Spirit gives light and hope to those of all faiths and of none. Let your blessing rest on those engaged in dialogue and action across many cultures. Grant them grace and sensitivity as they share together the riches of your love and seek the well-being of others. Amen.
*Donald Sampson, chaplain, St Mary's Hospice, Birmingham*

**Prison Prayer**
Jesus said, "I was hungry."
May those in prison taste and see that God is good.

Jesus said, "I was thirsty."
May those in prison who thirst for attention be refreshed by love.

Jesus said, "I was a stranger."
May those in prison know that they are welcome in your family.

Jesus said, "I was naked."
May all families of prisoners know that they are not alone.

Jesus said, "I was sick."
May all victims of crime get the support and access to justice that they need.

Jesus said, "I was in prison."
May staff and volunteers who work in prisons have the courage and perseverance to support those who feel abandoned. Amen.
*Bob Wilson, Free Churches Secretary for Prison Chaplaincy*

Lord, teach us that your Son died to save us, not from suffering but from ourselves; not from injustice, but from being unjust; and not from dying but so that we might die to ourselves; and this we ask through the same Christ our Lord. Amen.

*George MacDonald (1824-1905)*

**Tonga**
Methodist President
Finau Ahio

**Samoa**
Methodist President
Tupu Folasa

**Fiji**
Methodist President
Tuikilakila Waqairatu

**Scholarship Students**
Saimoni Vunilagi
(in Japan)
Sefanaia
Vuetikadavakimaiwai
Esala Nasaroa

Friendly God, we are thankful that we can hope in you and take refuge under your wings, for hope in you is all we have, and your light leads us on our journey to eternity.
We pray that you would grant your radiant light to **Tonga**'s leaders, and guide them to be hopeful disciples of your Son, Jesus Christ;
grant all the people of Tonga the strength of hope, and bless them as they seek light through darkness, and hope through hopelessness.
May the kingdom of Tonga be illumined by your presence now and forever.

*Fredrick Tui Feki, former SALT student from Tonga*

We give thanks for **Fiji** and all who live there and for God's mighty presence in the lives of Fiji's people over ages past and in years to come.
We pray for Fiji as it works towards democratic elections in 2014, the first since the military coup of December 2006; for the Methodist Church in Fiji and Rotuma under its new leaders, elected in August 2012: President Tuikilakila Waqairatu and General Secretary Tevita Bainivanua.

*Akuila Yabaki, Chief Executive Officer,*
*Citizens' Constitutional Forum, Fiji*

*Centenary Church of the Methodist Church in Tonga: a beacon of hope (Fredrick Tui Feki)*

Lord God,
    light in our darkness,
    hope in our despair,
may we remember each day that we are
    surrounded by your love,
    upheld by your power,
    possessed by your peace.
Thanks be to you. Amen.

*Peter Jarvis, supernumerary minister, Exeter*

We give thanks for the beauty of the Portadown District: the orchard county of Armagh, the rolling hills of Tyrone, the drumlins of Down and the little hills and lakes of Monaghan; for initiatives in the district to introduce people to Jesus; for hope in a border community emerging from a time of violence, that the darkness will remain in the past as the God of light leads his people into the future.
We pray for an outpouring of God's grace so that communities which were previously divided may build and work together; for everyone in the Portadown District who preaches the gospel, that their efforts will bear fruit and lives be enriched; for those from other nations who have come to live among the people of the district that the God of peace may take away their fear and enable them to settle, the God of love may help them to integrate and the God of life may prosper them.

**Portadown District (Ireland)**

Superintendent
Kenneth Robinson

---

We give thanks for the new circuit for the city of Sheffield and the surrounding area, and we pray for the continuing development of the life and mission of all circuits in the Sheffield District;
for people across the Sheffield District who live out their commitment to the gospel in their places of employment, in their communities and political life, at home and in their leisure pursuits and we pray for them;
for all who express compassion and look for justice in situations of deprivation across the Sheffield District.
We pray for those who struggle with poverty and for those in local government and in the voluntary and community sector who wrestle with hard choices as they seek to serve those in most need.

**Sheffield District**

Chair
Vernon Marsh

---

God, companion of all our travelling,
we thank you for the times when we walk in the light and all is clarity.
We thank you that you are with us when we are bewildered and lost in dark places.
Please shine your light on us, on the Church and on the way ahead;
and when we flinch from what we see, remind us that you love us
and that you call us to yourself from further down the road. Amen.

*Vernon Marsh, Sheffield District Chair*

Give us patience, O God, in the hour of trouble; humility in the hour of success and constancy in the hour of temptation. Grant us thankfulness for your benefits, fear of your judgement and hope in your enduring mercy; now and for ever. Amen.

*John Cosin (1594-1672)*

**The United Methodist Northern Europe Central Conference**

**NORDIC and BALTIC Area:**

**Bishop**
Christian Alsted

**Superintendents**
Denmark
Ole Birch
Keld Munk
Estonia
Taavi Hollman
Finland
*(Finnish language)*
Pasi Runonen
Finland
*(Swedish language)*
Björn Elfving
Mayvor Wärn-Rancken
Svein Veland
Latvia
Gita Mednis
Lithuania
William Lovelace
Norway
Øyvind Helliesen
Steinar Hjerpseth
Sweden
Bimbi Ollberg
Alf Englund
Thore Hildingsson

We pray for the new church in a former courtroom in Jokilaakso in Western **Finland**, that it will continue to grow and offer hope and grace in a depopulating area.

We give thanks for new beginnings for the United Methodist Church in Tallinn, **Estonia** where the young Church is reaching out particularly to people with drug addictions. We pray for people suffering in this way, and for their families, that God may give them strength to break out of their addiction and give them hope for a better future.

We give thanks for the International Methodist Church in Oslo, **Norway** (IMCO), which started at Pentecost 2012, one of many churches reaching out to the thousands of migrants coming to the Nordic countries in recent years.

We pray for the graduates of the Baltic Methodist Theological Seminary who will minister in the **Baltic States**, Finland and several other countries.

We give thanks that, through the UMC in the Nordic and Baltic countries, a supply of running water has been established to several villages in the Democratic Republic of Congo.

*Christian Alsted, Bishop,*
*United Methodist Church,*
*Nordic and Baltic area*

*New church in a former courtroom in Jokilaakso, Finland (Christian Alsted)*

*Biker ministry, Finland (Christian Alsted)*

*BMTS graduation, Estonia (Christian Alsted)*

**Southampton District**

Chair
Andrew Wood

We give thanks for the willingness of people in local churches and circuits to continue on the journey towards reshaping themselves for God's mission.

We remember those who are willing to let some things die in order that God's resurrection life may been seen in the communities whom they serve;

We give thanks for retreat space such as the Well Retreat for people who work with children and young people, which gives them a chance to reflect on their calling as Methodists in the Roots and Branches course.

We pray for the new circuits in Christchurch and Wimborne on the Isle of Wight, and Winchester and Eastleigh and the leadership teams which serve them;

for new initiatives and steps of faith: Messy Church, Saturday Church, Church with Choices which encourage people who did not imagine that church was for them;

for family and community workers and schools projects in Reading and Yeovil;

for the ministries of people who work in industry and commerce and for IBEX which enables industrial chaplaincy in the central south coast.

Lord of all,
Lord of the powerful, the power-hungry and the powerless;
Lord of the child, the childlike, and the child-abuser;
Lord of the lighthearted, the lightweight and the light-fingered;
Lord of the charming and the charmless, and those leading charmed lives;
Lord of the blessed, the blessing in disguise and the blessed nuisance;
Lord, whatever our starting point, take us, break us, remake us. Amen.

*Jenny Dyer, superintendent, Derby Circuit*

## Prayer for the beginning of a circuit meeting

God, make us ready to move within the light of your love, so that we may be open to the challenges which face our Church today. In the business of this meeting, and at all times, be with us in our speaking and in our thinking, that all our doing may always be for your glory. Amen.

*Eunice Page, local preacher, North Yorkshire Dales Circuit*

# DAY 27

Praying with Christians in Europe

Grant to us, O Lord, ears to hear your voice, eyes to see your beauty and hearts to love your name, so that hearing, seeing and loving we may come at last to the joys of your kingdom; through Christ our Lord. Amen.

*Christina Rossetti (1830-1894)*

**The United Methodist Northern Europe Central Conference (cont.)**

**EURASIA Area:**

**Russia**

Bishop
Eduard Khegay

**The United Methodist Central Conference of Germany**
Evangelisch-methodistische Kirche

Bishop
Rosemarie Wenner

**Mission Partners**
p  Barry° and Gillian Sloan, Michael and Megan

**Belgium**
Église Protestante Unie de Belgique

President
Steven Fuite

**France**
Église Protestante Unie de France

President
Laurent Schlumberger

Today we pray for all our sisters and brothers in **Eurasia**, from Kaliningrad in the west to Vladivostok in the east, from Archangelsk in the north to Sochi in the south.
We pray for the young generation of leaders, that they would mature as Christians and deepen and broaden their commitment to lead the nations;
for the many small and young churches, that they would be strengthened in their testimony and that they would spread personal and social holiness in their countries;
for all people of good will that they would be able to influence society towards greater openness and respect for people of all ethnicities and faiths.

*Hans Växby, former Bishop, United Methodist Church, Eurasia*

We thank God for the unity between the Reformed Church and the Evangelical Lutheran Church in **France** with the creation of the United Protestant Church of France in 2013.
We pray for United Churches around the world, that their unity may be a source of inspiration for other Churches and society as a whole, and strengthen peace and harmony between nations. We pray that through this march towards unity, the good news of Jesus Christ may be proclaimed and received.

*Didier Crouzet, International Relations Coordinator, United Protestant Church of France*

Lord Jesus Christ,
Son of God and light of the world,
you prayed that your disciples might all be one
so that the world might believe that the Father sent you.
Renew us by your Spirit
and, with our sisters and brothers and partner Churches,
send us to share with you in bringing hope to all the earth;
to the glory of your name. Amen.

*Neil Stubbens, Connexional Ecumenical Officer*

We give thanks to God for signs of hope:
 Godly Play in schools in Slaithwaite;
 the new mission bus in Calderdale;
 cooperation between the Study Centre in Rawalpindi and
  Touchstone in Bradford;
 the joint rural outreach initiatives of the Airedale, Settle, and
  Skipton and Grassington Circuits and
 the coming together of the Huddersfield and Holmfirth
  Circuits in 2013.
We pray for the continued work of the chaplaincies at the
Bradford Courts and Leeds-Bradford Airport;
the Blenheim Project, supporting victims of domestic violence;
the food drops and work with the homeless in Halifax, and
Denby Dale;
Fresh Expressions in North Kirklees and Morley, and many
other places in the district.

**West Yorkshire District**

Chair
Roger Walton

---

Gracious God, you are the hope of our journey and the light on our way.
Accompany us as we step forward in faith.
Be close to us as we seek to witness and serve.
When we flag, give us new energy;
when we are afraid, fresh courage;
when we feel overwhelmed, a sense of your enduring faithfulness;
and let our joy and delight in the gift of your love
shine from us to inspire hope in others. For Jesus' sake. Amen.

*Roger Walton, West Yorkshire District Chair*

---

Christ, be our hope
when sadness overwhelms us.
Christ, be our strength
when testing times are near.
Christ, be our light
when darkness would engulf us.
Christ, be our cornerstone
when quaking in our fear.
Christ, be our victory
when we lay our lives before you.
Christ, be our all-in-all,
today and evermore. Amen.

*Alison Judd, Area President (Britain and Ireland) of the World
Federation of Methodist and Uniting Church Women*

*Tree of life ...
tree of hope (logo of
the World Federation of
Methodist and Uniting
Church Women)*

O consuming fire, O spirit of love, descend into the depth of my heart and there transform me until I am fire of your fire, love of your love, and Christ himself is formed in me. Amen.

*Elizabeth of Schönau (d.1129-1165)*

**United Methodist Central and Southern Europe Central Conference**

**Bishop**
Patrick Streiff

**Superintendents**

Austria
Lothar Pöll

Bulgaria
Daniel Topalski

Czech Republic
Petr Procházka

Hungary
István Csernák

Poland
Andrzej Malicki
Józef Bartos
Sławomir Rodaszyński
Waldemar Eggert

Slovak Republic
Pavel Procházka

*Youthful hope in Alsozsolca, Hungary (Benjamin Sztupkai)*

We give thanks for the Roma congregation in Gorno Ezerovo, **Bulgaria** where more than 30 children attend Sunday School. We pray that the meeting of the Orthodox Universal Patriarchate and the World Methodist Council held in Bulgaria in September 2013 may serve to improve the relationship between the Bulgarian Orthodox Church and the United Methodist Church in Bulgaria.

*Daniel Topalski, Superintendent, Bulgaria*

We give thanks for social work with drug addicts, families, and young people undertaken by the United Methodist Church (UMC) in the **Czech Republic**.
We pray for the English-speaking UMC in Prague and for the mission among the English-speaking people of Prague; for missionary activities, for the opening of new churches and for the students at the Methodist Seminary in Prague.

*Petr Procházka, Superintendent, Czech Republic*

We give thanks for the opening of a new church in the Martha-Maria Home for the Elderly in Budakeszi, **Hungary**, that is also the home of the town's growing Methodist congregation; for the theology students who are willing and committed to serve in the UMC in Hungary.
We pray for money and the right personnel to continue the UMC's Roma ministry in Hungary.

*István Csernák, Superintendent, Hungary (translated by Eva Csernák)*

We give thanks for more than 90 years of Methodist witness on the Vistula River, **Poland** and for the longstanding Methodist radio and TV ministry through which the gospel and information on the UMC in Poland reaches many people;
We pray for young people and families who have decided to go abroad (mainly to Britain and Ireland) in order to find a job.

*Edward Puślecki, General Superintendent, Poland*

We give thanks for those engaged in chaplaincy, particularly for the Chaplaincy Project which is promoting lay chaplaincy; for the rural chaplaincy working among farmers and at livestock markets, and for town centre chaplains; for the pioneer ministry working among young people in Wolverhampton; for those who support and staff the District Children's Holiday and for the families who would otherwise have no holiday. We pray for the Tipton and West Bromwich Circuits as they join together as one this year; for the continuing work of the district project in Rwanda, for the newly trained Rwandan pastors, for the young people and adults from the district who take up the challenges of a visit to Rwanda and for the Church in Rwanda as it continues to work for reconciliation and harmony.

**Wolverhampton and Shrewsbury District**

Chair
John Howard

Dear God, we seek to reach out in mission,
to make a difference in your world today.
Sometimes what we can do for you seems insignificant.
Help us to recognise that
every time we help a person to feel wanted
we share your love;
every time we speak of our faith
we share a little of you;
and every time we work together to meet needs
we serve you.
Bless the work we do in mission. Amen.

*John Howard,*
*Wolverhampton and Shrewsbury District Chair*

## Prayer for the Leaders of Worship and Preachers Trust (LWPT)

Lord God, we ask for your guidance for the LWPT in their twin aims of offering the 'Best for worship' and the 'Best in time of need'. May your light shine on every aspect of the work of the LWPT so that practical hope and unconditional love can be offered to all who write, email or telephone the LWPT when they are worried or perplexed. Amen.

*Angela Davis, former chair,*
*Leaders of Worship and Preachers Trust*

> May the cross of the Son of God, mightier than all the powers of evil, bless our going out and our coming in. By the holy cross may we be delivered from all anger, all temptation and all unruly passion; and may almighty God bless us, the Father, the Son and the Holy Spirit, now and for ever. Amen.
>
> *Traditional Indian Liturgy*

**United Methodist Central and Southern Europe Central Conference (cont.)**

**Superintendents**

Algeria, Tunisia, France
Daniel Nussbaumer

Albania, Macedonia
Wilfried Nausner

Serbia
Ana Palik-Kunčak

Switzerland-France
Claudia Haslebacher
Jörg Niederer
Etienne Rudolph
Martin Streit

*Kabyle woman, Algeria (Daniel Nussbaumer)*

We give thanks for the men and women in **Algeria** who want to know more about Jesus, who get involved with a congregation and who – in many cases – want to be baptized even though they might face difficulties within their families because of their decision.

*Daniel Nussbaumer, Superintendent, Algeria/Tunisia*

Lord, in these times of political and economic tensions we ask that you would bring peace to the country of **Tunisia** and to the hearts of the people living there;
that the new study course for leaders will bear fruit;
for building work planned in Tunis-Montfleury, including the repair of the student hostel;
that your Church may be a living example of unity in Tunisian society.

*Freddy Nzambe, Tunisia*

We give thanks for the people in **Albania** who have recently started to live their lives in communion with Christ.
We pray for Mustafa Isufi and the United Methodist congregation in Pogradec who are looking for a new and bigger building;
for work with handicapped people in Tirana.

*Wilfried Nausner, Superintendent, Albania*

We give thanks for ongoing work with children in **Serbia**, such as Sunday Schools and special activities at Christmas and during the summer holidays.
We pray for all Christians in Serbia who face hostility and even persecution, that these experiences will work for their good, strengthening them and helping them to stand on solid ground.

*Ana Palik-Kunčak, Superintendent, Serbia*

We give thanks for continuing partnership across the Yorkshire Districts;

for the beauty of God's creation in the countryside, coast, towns and cities of Yorkshire;

for the friendship and support of all God's people in various traditions.

We pray for discernment in the development of the Discipleship and Ministries Learning Network across Yorkshire;

for patience and wisdom for those seeking to work with other Christians and all people of good will;

for deepening discipleship for all the people of the York and Hull District as they aim to be truly God's people.

**York and Hull District**

Chair
Stephen Burgess

*Whitby lighthouse
(© Photo.com, used
with permission)*

---

Compassionate and loving God, we pray for the bereaved and for those who feel sad and isolated. We remember them all, but especially those who have no close family or whose family are far away. We thank you, Lord, for Cruse volunteers and for pastoral visitors who are so privileged to be welcomed into people's homes. We pray that, as we empathise, listen and offer support, a spark of hope may be ignited in your name. Amen.

*Janet Stockley, Cruse volunteer and pastoral visitor, York*

---

*Lead, kindly light, amid the encircling gloom,*
*lead thou me on;*
loving and gracious God,
as a lighthouse sends out its beam
to guide and warn those who travel the seas,
so may the light of your presence guide and warn me throughout this day.
When the way ahead is unclear, or I am tempted to turn aside,
help me instead to turn to Jesus, the light of the world.
Help me to persevere, stage by stage, when the voyage is rough
and the destination far away;
    *I do not ask to see*
*the distant scene; one step enough for me.* Amen.

*inspired by John Henry Newman (1801-1890)*
**Stephen Burgess, York and Hull District Chair**

## Praying with Christians in Southern Europe

Be to us, O Holy Spirit, breath for our being, purity for our souls, healing for our wounds, fire for our hearts and light for our path, that with all creation we may rejoice in your presence; now and for ever. Amen.

*Hildegard of Bingen (1098-1179)*

**Portugal**
Igreja Evangelica
Metodista Portuguesa

**Bishop**
Sifredo Teixeira

**Scholarship Student**
Ana Cristina Aco
(in Brazil)

**Spain**
Iglesia Evangelica
Española

**President**
Joel Cortés

**Italy**
Opera per le Chiese
Evangeliche Metodiste
in Italia (OPCEMI)

**Methodist President**
Alessandra Trotta

**Mission Partners**
p Ken° and Marion
Howcroft

**Conference of
European Churches**

**General Secretary**
Guy Liagre

**Community of
Protestant Churches
in Europe**

**Central Secretary**
Michael Bünker

We give thanks for the many blessings received by the Evangelical Methodist Church in **Portugal**;
for the solidarity centres where the Church supports children, families and the elderly;
for the new building for the local church in Lisbon which has been made possible by the city's mayor;
for the new group of Angolan Methodists who are bringing life and joy to the Church in Porto;
for the new discipleship programme in Porto which started with the support of the Brazilian Methodist Church.
We pray for those who are facing difficult situations because of health problems and unemployment, and those who are worried about what will happen during this time of austerity where there seems to be bad news every day.

*Sifredo Teixeira, Bishop,
Portuguese Evangelical Methodist Church*

Gracious God, we ask your blessing on the Methodist women of **Italy** as they prepare to host the Joint Area Seminar in Pomezia, near Rome in June 2014. We give thanks for this opportunity for women from Britain, Ireland and many European nations to share together and learn from each other as they seek to "know Christ and make him known". Amen.

*Alison Judd, Area President (Britain and Ireland),
World Federation of Methodist and Uniting Church Women*

We give thanks for signs of growth in the Methodist Church in Florence and for developing and deepening relationships with the other Florentine Protestant churches;
for the multicultural witness of the Italian Methodist Church.
We pray for the ongoing work of cultural integration in Italy as a nation and within the Churches;
for clarity in moments of misunderstanding which arise between cultures and generations.

*Alison Walker, former mission partner, Italy*

We give thanks for the opportunities for deepening discipleship in worship and small groups; for sharing faith through VentureFX projects in the Inverness and the Edinburgh and Forth Circuits and Alpha groups on the Moray Coast; for those continuing to put into effect the vision for resourcing local churches and outlying groups through district development.
We pray for the three presbyters new to the district that, together with other dedicated lay and ordained leaders, they will strengthen the work of the Church in its national and ecumenical setting; for the furthering of local churches' engagement in the wider community, particularly through opportunities during the Commonwealth Games in Scotland in 2014.

### Scotland District

**Chair**
David Easton

*Renewal of rigs in winter sunshine, River Tay, Dundee harbour (David Easson)*

God of hope, I thank you that my future is in your hands and for your patient, powerful presence in my life. I am sorry for my failure to place my trust in your goodness and mercy. I offer you now my whole heart, mind, body and soul; and ask you to continue to empower me with your forgiveness and love. Amen.
*Hilary Henderson, Scotland District Local Preachers and Worship Leaders Secretary*

Almighty God, we thank you that you provide resources, both local and connexional, for the Methodist Church in Shetland. We praise you for those whose prayers sustain, protect and inspire us.
We bless you for opportunities for sharing the love of Jesus in the Shetland community.
Dear God, we pray for the continuing building of your kingdom in the lives of children and young people in Shetland's churches and community; for the children and youth worker, and all those involved in ministry to young people.

### Shetland District

**Chair**
Jeremy Dare

This day we would live our lives for you,
    please help us move our dreams to reality.
This day we would like to show your holy grace,
    please help us to walk closely with you.
This day we would like to inspire hope,
    please help us to trust in your promises. Amen.
*Jeremy Dare, Shetland District Chair*

Come Holy Spirit, fill our thoughts that we may see all things through your eyes; awaken our souls that we may love all things with your tenderness; and melt our hearts that we may feel all things with your compassion; through Christ our Lord. Amen.

*Johann Freylinghausen (1670-1739)*

**Mission partners and others recently returned from overseas:**

**2012/2013**

Julia Edwards (Fiji)

David Furnival (Nepal)

Chris and Vera Lacey, Sofie and Abigail (Antigua, MCCA)

Helen Moorehead (Kenya)

Maggie Patchett (Belize)

James and Dipty Linda Pender (Bangladesh)

Eddie and Susan Sykes, (Bahamas, MCCA)

Alison and Robin Walker (Italy)

David and Sarah Hall, Rebecca, Reuben and Matthew (Bangladesh)

**Ecumenical Accompaniers who served in 2013**

John Howard

Jenny Bywaters

Gracious God, we pray for those who have recently returned from working in another country.

We thank you for all that can be gained by their experiences, both by the individuals themselves and by those who listen to their stories.

We give thanks that ties of love are not constrained by geographical distance,

we remember the bonds of love and friendship made in other countries, and are grateful that communication is easier than it was in the time of our forebears.

We pray for those who have lost loved ones while they were away, and for those who struggle with the bereavement of leaving another country and place of work.

We pray that those who receive them back will be open to listening to them and trying to understand and support them in order to help them readjust to a different way of life.

We thank you that you are a God who journeys with us, in our goings-out and comings-in.

*Rosemary Fletcher, former mission partner, Sri Lanka*

Universal God, we give thanks for the work of the World Mission Forum and for its members, who represent all parts of our Connexion.

We thank you that we can delight and be confident in the knowledge that we belong to the worldwide Methodist Church, a Church filled with hope and holiness.

We pray for the forum's gatherings that, through sharing, learning and policy consultations, all participants will be empowered by the light of Christ to spread good news and bring hope to their local situations.

We pray for the World Church Relationships Team, that they will feel sustained and supported by the whole of the British Methodist Connexion, confident that the God of hope is travelling with them as they seek to share his love with our partner Churches across the world.

*Frances Hopwood, secretary, World Mission Forum*

## Celebrating 200 years of Methodist missionary work

For Nathaniel Gilbert in Antigua who started the first Methodist society beyond the British Isles;
for Thomas Coke from Brecon who helped plant the gospel in America, the Caribbean, Africa and Asia;
for the visionaries in Leeds who, in 1813, founded the first missionary society to support Methodist preachers abroad;
for soldiers, settlers and missionaries who shared their faith far from home;
for all those in many places who heard God's call and became co-workers in Christ's service;
for the initiatives of the Methodist Missionary Society over two centuries;
for the people who inspired and supported them with prayer, gifts and enthusiasm,
and for those who took the risks and the opportunities of mission in other lands, thanks be to God.

*John Pritchard, minister, Hassocks*

We remember the World Council of Churches (WCC) and pray for the tenth WCC Assembly held from 30 October to 8 November 2013 in Busan, South Korea and all that flows from it.

*Neil Stubbens, Connexional Ecumenical Officer*

*Let the groans of the prisoners come before you.*
Lord, as we pray with the World Council of Churches for persecuted Christians, awaken your people around the world to their suffering. Stir us to pray for our fellow Christians in deepest solidarity. Empower the efforts of organisations such as Christian Solidarity Worldwide and Release International. Increase their ability to lobby both national governments and supranational organisations such as the United Nations and European Union. Inspire more churches to form support groups that will pray, send cards to those in prison and raise money for the organisations that help our persecuted brothers and sisters in their need.

*inspired by Psalm 79:11*
*John Sennett, local preacher, Chislehurst*

## World Church Relationships

**Leader**
David Friswell

**Partnership Coordinators:**
Africa
Olubunmi Olayisade
Americas
Sandra Lopez
Asia-Pacific
Steve Pearce
Europe
Roy Crowder

## World Methodist Council (WMC)

**General Secretary**
Ivan Abrahams

*As a member of the WMC the Methodist Church in Britain also relates to other Methodist Churches worldwide. For a full list please see the WMC website www.worldmethodist council.org*

## World Council of Churches (WCC)

**General Secretary**
Olav Fykse Tveit

*The WCC is a fellowship of 349 Churches, denominations and church fellowships in more than 110 countries and territories throughout the world, representing over 560 million Christians.*

# Additional Resources

A Gift of Prayer, a small treasury of prayers from around the world based on the Lord's Prayer. Available in packs of 50, priced £5 (plus p&p) from Methodist Publishing, tel: 01733 235962 or www.methodistpublishing.org.uk

A Word in Time, www.methodist.org.uk/bible offers commentary on the daily readings from the Prayer Handbook.

Deepening Discipleship, www.methodist.org.uk/deepeningdiscipleship, provides resources for individual and small group reflection to help you deepen your faith and develop your discipleship with God.

Magnet, a contemporary Christian magazine, with thoughtful meditation pages, seasonal worship resources, insightful features, Bible study and prayer focus. For more information, contact Lynne Ling, tel: 0845 250 0509, email: lynne.magnet@gmail.com

Mission Matters, www.methodist.org.uk/missionmatters, contains information, resources and stories from Britain and the World Church.

Prayer and Care, a regularly updated leaflet from Methodists in World Mission containing news and prayer requests from mission partners working across the world and in Britain. Available from www.mwm.org.uk/prayer-and-care

Prayer Focus, the Prayer Handbook of the Methodist Church in Ireland available from the Methodist Church in Ireland, No 9 Resources Centre, 9 Lennoxvale, Belfast BT9 5BY.

The Methodist Recorder, from your newsagent or 122 Golden Lane, London EC1Y 0TL.

The Prayer Handbook on CD, from Galloways Society for the Blind, Howick House, Howick Park Avenue, Penwortham, Preston PR1 0LS, tel: 01772 753705.

The Upper Room Daily Devotional guide, available from BRF, 15 The Chambers, Vineyard, Abingdon OX14 3FE, tel: 01865 319700, email: enquiries@brf.org.uk.

World Church Relationships Bulletin, sign up through www.methodist.org.uk/signup, to receive a monthly newsletter packed with news from overseas partners, mission partners and more.

HOPE, an invitation to local mission in 2014. Ideas for how you might be able to engage your local community, in partnership with other Christians, are available in the HOPE resource book 'Hope Heartbeat' (£5.99 per copy) and at www.hopetogether.org.uk.

Key – the letters beside the names indicate the type of work in which mission partners are mainly engaged:

ad administration
d doctor
ed education
m medical work (other than doctor or nurse)
n nurse
p pastoral worker
rt retired
sd social/development work
t technical
th theological training
° minister
+ Joint Appointment
CMS Church Mission Society (Anglican)
CofS Church of Scotland
CWM Council for World Mission

**Other Abbreviations**

SALT Scholarship and Leadership Training
WCR World Church Relations
UMC United Methodist Church